"In a world that seems to be going crazy, finding meaningful work that not only pays the bills but helps people and society and the earth to heal is becoming more important than ever. What do I really want to do with my life? How can I make a difference? Maia's insightful book shows us how to approach those questions, in a way that can help us discover our own true path."

— David Loy, *A New Buddhist Path*

"As Lao Tzu said, 'A journey of a thousand miles begins with one step' and reading this book might well be yours. For anyone who's spent time looking for a way to love what they do, Maia Duerr charts a step-by-step route for getting there. Wise, realistic, and encouraging."

— Karen Maezen Miller, author of *Paradise in Plain Sight* and *Hand Wash Cold*

"This is a clear and wonderful guide on how to bring balance and wisdom into your livelihood."

— Roshi Joan Jiko Halifax, Abbot of Upaya Zen Center, *The Fruitful Darkness*

"*Work That Matters* counsels us on how to optimize not only our work life but life itself. This helpful book offers the reader a way to look deeply, discover, and creatively follow our true-life direction. Becoming intimate with our core intention, the way opens, and we can discern our unique path to rewarding and meaningful work. The concrete exercises and reflections Maia offers will lead to a transformation of the meaning and value of your work choices."

— Roshi Pat Enkyo O'Hara, *Most Intimate*

"The most creative contributions to this world are usually made by people who have aligned their work with their deepest values and true intentions. I have worked with Maia Duerr in many contexts and have witnessed her commitment to cultivating this awareness and finding skillful ways to teach it to others. This is not just another book on mindfulness—it could change every working day of your life."
— Mirabai Bush, Senior Fellow of the Center for Contemplative Mind in Society, *Working with Mindfulness*

"Maia Duerr brings a mindful and liberating approach to creating a work life that speaks to one's unique gifts and purpose. Providing key tools and exercises, this gem of a book can help you navigate a path from an unfulfilling job to a meaningful and joyful career of your own making."
— Brenda Salgado, *Real World Mindfulness for Beginners*

"This wise and brilliant book harnesses the power of mindfulness and a host of creative and visionary techniques and practices to help you find the work that you love. Maia Duerr is an insightful, compassionate, and experienced guide along the way. This book will change your life."
—Diana Winston, Director of Mindfulness Education at UCLA's Mindful Awareness Research Center, coauthor *Fully Present*

"If you want to find joy in your work, read this book! Maia Duerr is the kindest and most encouraging of guides. She helps us look into our own hearts to clarify what matters to us, and points us toward practical tools that can help us manifest this vision. This book will be helpful to anyone who is considering their work at any stage of life. I found myself eagerly doing the exercises at the end of each chapter, and was reminded of priorities of my own that I have been neglecting. Now in my mid-seventies, my own work life has been enriched. This book about finding a fulfilling livelihood is essential and straight from the heart."
—Susan Moon, *This is Getting Old*

WORK
THAT
MATTERS

To Ellen,
May you always
have work
that matters!

Maia

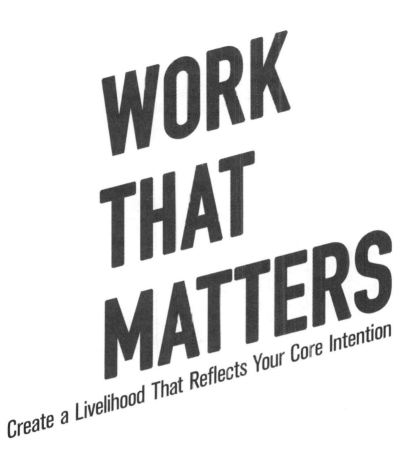

WORK
THAT
MATTERS

Create a Livelihood That Reflects Your Core Intention

MAIA DUERR

Foreword by PAMELA SLIM

 **PARALLAX PRESS**

BERKELEY, CALIFORNIA

Parallax Press
P. O. Box 7355
Berkeley, CA 94707
parallax.org

Parallax Press is the publishing division of Plum Village Community
of Engaged Buddhism, Inc.
© 2017 Maia Duerr
All rights reserved
Printed in the United States of America

Cover and text design by John Barnett / www.4eyesdesign.com
Cover photos © Shutterstock
Illustrations of meditation poses © Terri Saul
The Tree of Contemplative Practices illustration appears courtesy of
The Center for Contemplative Mind in Society
Author photograph © Genevieve Russell

Library of Congress Cataloging-in-Publication Data

Names: Duerr, Maia, author.
Title: Work that matters : create a livelihood that reflects your core
    intention / Maia Duerr ; foreword by Pamela Slim.
Description: Berkeley, Califorinia : Parallax Press. [2017]
Identifiers: LCCN 2017023669 (print) | LCCN 2017036991 (ebook) |
ISBN
    9781941529683 | ISBN 9781941529683
Subjects: LCSH: Vocational guidance. | Job satisfaction. | Quality of work
    life.
Classification: LCC HF5381 (ebook) | LCC HF5381 .D823 2017 (print)
| DDC
    650.1--dc23
LC record available at https://lccn.loc.gov/2017023669

1 2 3 4 5 / 21 20 19 18 17

To Nicole Sangsuree Barrett ... this book
would have been my gift to you, if you'd been
able to stay around long enough to see it.
As it is, you're doing the work that matters
most from the realm of the stars. Thank
you for shining your brilliant light on all of
us and for being a huge inspiration to me
during your short time on this planet.

CONTENTS

Foreword by Pamela Slim   8
How to Use This Book   12

PART I: FOUNDATIONS   16

Chapter 1: A Love Story about Work   18
Chapter 2: What Is Liberation-Based Livelihood?   26
Chapter 3: Three Building Blocks of Transformation   34

    1. Returning to This Very Moment   36
    2. Leveraging Adversity   44
    3. Staying the Course   46

PART II: THE 6 KEYS TO LIBERATION-BASED LIVELIHOOD 50

Chapter 4: Key 1: Become Intimate with Your Core Intention   52
Chapter 5: Key 2: Value Your Gifts and Time   74
Chapter 6: Key 3: Break Through Inertia and Take Action   92
Chapter 7: Key 4: Make Friends with Uncertainty   106
Chapter 8: Key 5: Think Big and Make the
                 Most of Your Resources   118
Chapter 9: Key 6: Build a Circle of Allies and Ask for Help 134

PART III: NAVIGATIONAL TOOLS 148

Chapter 10: Craft Your Personal Mission Statement 150
Chapter 11: Strategies and Tools for Navigating the Three
Pathways to Liberation-Based Livelihood 164

1. Plan Your Exit Strategy 166
2. Love the Job You've Got 171
3. Create Work That You Love 182

Chapter 12: Create Your Personal Action Plan 196
Conclusion: True Freedom through Work That Matters 208

Notes 212
Resources 216
Appendices

A. Loving Kindness Practice 224
B. Guide to Creating a Personal Retreat 227
C. Treasure Hunting Letter Example 232
Acknowledgments 234
About the Author 237

FOREWORD

I sat in the darkroom on a stool next to my dad, watching him look through a page of contact sheets with a handheld magnifying glass.

"There—look at the difference between these two photos. What do you notice?"

I squinted as I looked between the two images. They were so similar, but then I noticed that in one, the person on the far left had a slightly different look on her face. Her eyes looked brighter and her smile felt more genuine. I could sense how the picture worked better than the nearly identical one next to it.

"This one looks slightly better. That look on her face does it."

I watched a quiet smile spread on his face.

"That's right. That's why you have to take so many pictures. There are always slight inconsistencies, or things that feel a tiny bit off. Out of the two hundred pictures you take to get one shot, you will find the one that works. I am always relieved when I find it."

Perhaps you have been lucky enough to witness someone doing work that they love. For some, it is expressed as working calmly and thoughtfully on their craft. For others, you feel the passion pouring out of them as they cook up a storm, or speak or teach with great enthusiasm.

These people love their work. They are devoted to their work. It feeds them and fuels them. Who doesn't want that?

Finding out what you want to be when you grow up, or how to make money from your passions, or what your next job or career is, or how to make meaning from your time on Earth are questions that many, many people ask themselves.

Imagine how wonderful life would be if you enjoyed the things you did to put food on your table.

So why is it so hard?

When you are in a state of flux with work, it feels like it will never get better. You have so many thoughts happening simultaneously:

- "Why can't I just be happy with what I have? It is a solid, stable job. Most people would be so grateful to have this work situation."

- "I could never make money with my passion. It is totally unrealistic."
- "I have no idea what I want to do. I am just totally stumped."
- "I want to make a positive impact on the world. It seems like all the jobs that generate decent money are involved in greed or exploitation of some kind."

Doubt and frustration and overwhelm creep in, and it can be totally paralyzing. We start to blame ourselves:

- "Why can't I figure this out?"
- "So many of my friends seem to have it together. What is wrong with me?"

There are a lot of differing views about what you should do to solve your work dilemma:

- "Searching for passion in your work will get you nowhere. Find a decent job that funds your dreams, and suck it up."
- "Set up an online business and outsource everything. Watch the money roll in while you cavort on a beach somewhere."

All the different approaches, ideas, and expectations start to add to your confusion and overwhelm. Before you know it, you are shrinking from the quest for meaningful work, and you spiral into fear and inaction.

There is a lot of romanticizing about ideal businesses or careers. We long for an instant blueprint or result from a report that tells us what our perfect career or business looks like.

The Alternative

What if it didn't have to work this way?

What if instead of looking at a sea of career options in the outside world you took a calm, introspective, and deliberate approach to finding your right livelihood?

What if you learned how to tune in deeply to your own voice and wisdom?

What if you accepted that this journey did not have to be a neat, orderly package, but rather a deeply meaningful, transformational adventure that was full of insight and emotion and reflection?

In *Work That Matters*, Maia introduces a powerful process of exploration that veers from common approaches to career development.

A Liberation-Based Livelihood is exactly as it sounds—a process of getting free from unhelpful thoughts and stories about yourself, of obstacles and limitations, and of lack of possibilities.

It embraces the philosophy that your work does not have to be disconnected from your values. Your success does not have to impede someone else's rights. Your work can make you free, and contribute to others' freedom in the process.

Your Liberation-Based Livelihood is going to look very different from anyone else's.

You may find, as Maia did on her own path, that your work journey will involve many different jobs or roles along the way.

Or you may find, as my dad did with photography, a singular craft that you can grow with over many decades, deepening your mastery and perspective.

Do the Work

In all the years that I have been a career coach, the only distinguishing characteristic between those who find meaningful work and those who struggle is the willingness to engage in the process, no matter how uncomfortable or challenging it can be at points along the way.

You could not have chosen a better guide for your journey than Maia. Take the time to practice her mindfulness techniques. They will wake up ideas and possibilities you never considered.

Do your reflection and research. The process of unearthing ideas and looking for patterns will give you unique insight into your special genius.

Take action and ask for help. You do not have to do this journey alone.

What waits on the other side is my wish and prayer for everyone: deeply meaningful and nourishing work that lights you up, fulfills your needs, and makes the world a safer, more just, healthy, free, and equitable place.

Let's get started!

—Pamela Slim, author,
Escape from Cubicle Nation and *Body of Work*
Mesa, Arizona, July 2017

HOW TO USE THIS BOOK

There is no outer prescription, course, or exercise that will bring a person to good work. We find it from the inside out.... Every one of us has the responsibility and the capability to construct his or her own map of reality and to dream, think, and act on the basis of it—then reflect on the action and its consequences to strengthen and make more fruitful the succeeding cycles of dreaming and thinking and acting.

—E. F. Schumacher

If you've been searching for work that doesn't just pay your bills but that you can truly fall in love with, this book is for you. It's the book I wish I'd had about twenty years ago, as I tried to find my way out of a lot of career-related suffering.

Perhaps, like me, you've tried many strategies to find work that matters—career counseling, aptitude tests, reading other books on the topic, and more. If you feel stuck and have been unable to gain traction in this part of your life, the mindfulness-based approach that's at the heart of this book can help you make a shift at a deeper level that creates possibilities for new insights and positive change. I've witnessed this process of transformation unfolding many times in the lives of the folks who have gone through my online course, "Fall in Love with Your Work," upon which this book is based.

Here's the most important thing you need to know right from the start: this book works from the inside out.

You are about to embark on a journey that invites you to go deep within yourself to get reacquainted with parts of your heart and mind you may have lost touch with. From my own experience, these hidden areas are the necessary ingredients to access that level of consciousness where transformation can take place—in this case, a transformation in your relationship to your work. In the first two chapters, I'll tell you a little bit about myself and share the story of how I found my way from extreme job burnout to creating a livelihood that I truly love. Following this "inside out" approach, we'll then practice the three building blocks to transformation in chapter 3: returning to this very moment, leveraging adversity, and staying the course.

We won't stay exclusively in the inward-looking self-reflection realm because if you're like most of us, you need to figure out how to make a living! And there are some clear action steps you can take to make that possible. If you engage wholeheartedly with this book, you'll find yourself in a vibrant dance between dreaming and thinking and acting, as E. F. Schumacher beautifully describes above.

But the heart of this approach, based in moment-to-moment awareness, invites you to focus on the internal qualities, beliefs, and attitudes that you need to cultivate in order to create work that truly sustains you, in every sense of the word. This is what I call "Liberation-Based Livelihood."

In my experience, there are six "keys" that make Liberation-Based Livelihood possible:
1. Become Intimate with Your Core Intention
2. Value Your Gifts and Time
3. Break Through Inertia and Take Action
4. Make Friends with Uncertainty
5. Think Big and Make the Most of Your Resources
6. Build a Circle of Allies and Ask for Help

In the first half of the book we'll explore these 6 Keys in depth and you'll work through explorations and practices designed to strengthen your capacity for each one. The sequence of these Keys is quite intentional; I encourage you to move through them in the order they are presented. At the same time, there is a synergy between the Keys. For example, you may discover that by increasing your comfort level with uncertainty (Key 4), you will strengthen your ability to take action (Key 3). Rather than thinking of them as a linear path, it might be helpful to understand that they function in more of an interrelated, circular way. Another secret that reveals itself as you go through the book is that these keys can apply to more than your work—they offer a tried-and-true map for living a wholehearted life.

Creating a Liberation-Based Livelihood pivots on your Personal Mission Statement, which you'll create in chapter 10. This statement will be informed by the insights you gain as you move through the 6 Keys, particularly the first one.

In the last part of the book, you'll play more in the realm of "acting" as you discover other tangible ways to bring your Liberation-Based Livelihood into reality and as you design your Personal Action Plan.

The whole process is a lot like putting together a jigsaw puzzle. As you become familiar with the 6 Keys and make your way through the exercises, you may have "a-ha!" moments when you find that corner piece you had been missing, and then the rest of the puzzle gradually comes together in ways that surprise and delight you.

While you could, in theory, quickly zoom through each exercise, this is designed to be a mindfulness-based process, so I encourage you to take your time and ground each exploration in your own contemplative practice, whether through meditation, creativity, breathing exercises, etc. (If you don't have a practice, you'll learn how to begin one in chapter 3, "Three Building Blocks of Transformation.") For example, as you move through "Mining for Gold" in chapter 4, take breaks between each section and do some yoga or sitting meditation or whatever practice is nourishing for you. Then return to the exercise from that more relaxed mind-set and notice what happens.

You may find it helpful to start a journal where you gather the insights that emerge as you go through this process, and where you can jot down the ideas that begin to come to you about your Liberation-Based Livelihood.

This book can be just the start of your journey! Please connect with me through our online community at my website, maiaduerr.com/work-that matters, where you'll find additional resources and invitations to join ongoing discussions with others about how to create Liberation-Based Livelihood. I look forward to hearing your experiences as you undertake this journey. May it be fruitful and beneficial to you, as well as benefit all beings, with whom we are interconnected.

PART I
Foundations

CHAPTER 1 A Love Story about Work

The work of the world is common as mud.
Botched, it smears the hands, crumbles to dust.
But the thing worth doing well done
has a shape that satisfies, clean and evident.
Greek amphoras for wine or oil,
Hopi vases that held corn, are put in museums
but you know they were made to be used.
The pitcher cries for water to carry
and a person for work that is real.

—Marge Piercy

I'm ten years old and sitting at the dining room table with Mom waiting for Dad to come home from work. He's always late. By the time he sits down to dinner, the food has cooled off, despite Mom's best attempts to keep it warm. Once the mealtime conversation starts, much of it revolves around Dad's discontent with his job. He feels perpetually overworked and stays long hours to try to catch up—hence his tardiness to dinner. He complains endlessly about his boss. I sit there and witness my Dad's unhappiness and feel heartbroken. And I wonder … does it have to be this way?

My father worked as a travel counselor for the American Automobile Association, a job he chose because of his own love of travel. He was the guy who would give you maps for your vacation and point out the things you shouldn't miss along with the way, like the amazing natural rock bridge in Utah that nobody else knew about, or the quirky motel in Nevada that doubled as a peacock farm.

Dad spent all his time and energy planning other people's trips but rarely had time to take one himself. It seemed to me that he lived only for his vacation time—two weeks a year, the standard amount of annual vacation in the United States. He held that job for more than thirty years until he finally retired in his late sixties.

My dad's experience and perspective were not unusual. Most of my friends' parents had similarly limited time off and expressed the same sentiments. As I grew up and then got my first job, the general consensus among my friends was that work was something to be endured rather than enjoyed.

Early on, I vowed that my life would be different, that I would do whatever it took not simply to tolerate my work but to find joy in it. I wanted my livelihood to be a vehicle for my personal and spiritual growth, and a way for me to give something back to the world. This vow has led me on a wild and woolly adventure over the past thirty years through at least five careers and twenty jobs (and I am being conservative in these estimates). Over this period of time, some of the positions I've held (or created) have included the following:

- Kentucky Fried Chicken counterperson
- alfalfa sprout packer
- administrative assistant
- music therapist
- mental health counselor
- bookseller
- freelance writer
- cultural anthropologist
- research director
- nonprofit executive director
- communications director
- magazine editor
- project manager
- organizational consultant
- buddhist minister/chaplain
- meditation teacher

How in the world do I make sense out of that list? While I do feel some pride in all these job adventures and the fact that I haven't followed a conventional path, sometimes I look at this list and wonder, "What the hell am I doing with my life?" I wonder if I've skimmed the surface of too many occupations without staying in something long enough to be an "expert." Sometimes I envy people who seem to know exactly what they want to do when they were ten years old and then stay on a steady trajectory to become a doctor or lawyer or something else more clearly defined. This clearly has not been my path.

At times, I still fall into the trap of comparing myself to folks like that and buy into social expectations about what a career "should" look like. When that happens it can be easy to feel like a "failure." But with a positive reframe, I realize that I'm actually a Renaissance woman with diverse skills, and that I've made these career changes over the years in response to the changing circumstances of my life as well as growing clarity about what I'm here on the planet to offer.

I'm not alone in this pattern. The new world of work is a very different environment from the one in which my father grew up. According to a 2015 study by the Bureau of Labor Statistics, each of us will hold 11.7 jobs over our lifetime. On average, a US worker has been in his or her current job 4.4 years—a dramatic drop from the 1970s, when it wasn't unusual for people to have careers that lasted fifteen or twenty years.[1]

It turns out that creating a career in the twenty-first century is less about a job title and more about the life mission that we've discerned for ourselves. As author and business coach Pamela Slim writes, "The new world of work requires a new lens and skill set to ensure career success.... When you view your career through the lens of an overarching body of work, you know the deeper roots that connect your entire work and life experience."[2]

When I reflect on my own body of work, I see that the first time I began to apply this kind of lens came near the end of career number one as a mental health worker. The younger version of me thought I had done everything "right" in setting up that career. I chose to pursue a bachelor's degree in music therapy because that seemed in line with what I thought I should be doing: helping people. The musical part of my job added a creative twist, which was also in tune with my personality. What could go wrong?

I started out as a music therapist in a Connecticut state psychiatric hospital. After three years in that job, I worked in various other positions in the mental health system. It took me ten years before I was finally able to acknowledge how unhappy I was doing that work. Not all of it—I loved engaging with my patients and clients, yet even these interactions could be challenging and stressful. But as time went on, I became disillusioned by the failings of a system that was charged with caring for people's mental health but often did exactly the opposite and proved toxic to almost everyone involved: patients, their families, and staff. In addition, I felt frustrated and constrained by the way in which my jobs affected the structure of my life. (Showing up at 8:00 a.m. every day? An hour-long commute to work? Please....)

But the thought of letting it all go and doing something else was terrifying. After all, I had invested ten years of my life in this profession, and I was getting paid pretty well. I watched as my colleagues took the next logical step and became supervisors and administrators, some of them going back to school for an MSW or PhD. In the mental health profession this was the conventional career track.

I looked at MSW programs and started to apply for a few of them. Yet something inside me resisted mightily and I couldn't even finish the applications. I was at war with myself. What it took to finally step out of this war zone was an honest recognition of how depleted I was— physically, emotionally, and spiritually.

Out of desperation, I started making a list of the things I truly enjoyed doing, activities that brought me happiness. I had an idea that this might give me a clue about my next career step.

My list included the following:

- travel
- meeting people from different cultures
- listening to people's stories
- writing

The seeds of these things that I loved to do were present in my mental health positions. Working with patients with psychiatric disabilities and in extreme emotional states was similar in some ways to being with people from another culture, as I had to step out of myself and learn to understand their unique ways of navigating the world. I also had to write up clinical notes after each visit or session. But rather than simply bearing witness to another's story and holding space for their healing, I was part of a team that would give them a diagnosis such as schizophrenia or bipolar disorder. This label might result in helping them access treatment, but more often than not became a source of stigma (and too often the treatments were ineffective and even harmful). All of this was eating away at me.

I made a number of efforts to figure out if there was a career path better suited to me. I read books like *What Color is Your Parachute?* and *Do What You Love, The Money Will Follow.* I went to a career counselor and took aptitude tests. (The results of one test indicated I should be a lawyer, which I doubt would have been a good move for me!) Each of these strategies offered a few helpful insights, but something wasn't clicking on a deeper level.

At some point during that period of intense questioning, when I was in my early thirties, I had the good fortune of participating in a retreat on Whidbey Island, Washington. One of the retreat faculty was Dr. Angeles Arrien, an inspiring cultural anthropologist and writer. One day I found time to have an individual conversation with Dr. Arrien. As we walked amidst the emerald green fields of the retreat center, she encouraged me to look into the graduate program that she had cofounded in San Francisco. Something inside me lit up as I reviewed my list of "things I love" and realized that each of them was related to things an anthropologist might do. I had absolutely no idea how one would make a living as an anthropologist—the only role model I could think of was the hopelessly stereotyped, unrealistic image of Indiana Jones—but I was willing to take a big leap to get myself out of the work-related suffering I had been stuck in for so long.

It also helped to have encouragement from friends who could see how dissatisfied I was and who knew I had gifts to offer that weren't being expressed through my work.

That combination—identifying my gifts, being exposed to other possibilities, receiving encouragement, being willing to make a leap—made a big shift possible. (As you may notice, they are also an early version of the 6 Keys that you'll explore in this book.)

At thirty-two years old, I finally had the courage and clarity to end my ten-year career in mental health, and I entered the Social and Cultural Anthropology Program at the California Institute of Integral Studies (CIIS) in San Francisco. Sometimes I think of this decision as my "Hail Mary pass," as it took a tremendous leap of faith as well as finances. I had saved a bit of money but had to take out a great deal of student loans to make graduate school possible.

During that period of time, I also started a meditation practice, first with Roshi Joan Halifax (whom I met when she taught a course on Buddhism, Shamanism, and Deep Ecology at CIIS), and then with Vietnamese Zen Master Thich Nhat Hanh's Community of Mindful Living sangha in the San Francisco Bay Area. *Sangha* is a Sanskrit word that means "community"; in Buddhism, people recognize that individuals need a group of like-minded friends around them to make progress on a spiritual path. The combination of study at CIIS and my entry into meditation provided me with a new way of viewing the world and practices to help stabilize my mind and open my heart.

That experience of making a major career change provided the seeds for what later became an online course called "Fall in Love with Your

Work," which I created in 2012. My mindfulness practice has provided a foundation of self-awareness from which I can make choices about work that are informed by wisdom rather than reactivity. This is the same process I will share with you in this book.

Through my own mindful inquiry over the past decade, I discovered that the myriad jobs I've held are all actually a manifestation of one thing, my Core Intention: a deep desire to help people discover their passions and connect with one another. (Though I'm not sure how the alfalfa sprout job would fit with this!) You'll learn more about how to find your own Core Intention in chapter 4.

Once my Core Intention became clear, I felt a tremendous sense of relief. It was as though the numbers on a padlock all clicked into place, unlocking a clarity that has helped me to seek out increasingly fulfilling work opportunities. I no longer felt in danger of becoming like my father and seeing work as something to be endured rather than enjoyed.

As I've become more conscious of my Core Intention, I've strengthened my ability to align my work with it. I've also learned how to think "out of the box" and not rely on anyone else's definition of "job" to limit how I do this. The outcome has been fascinating and not where I ever thought I would end up. I've created a livelihood with which I support people to "discover" and "connect" by doing the things I love to do the best: listening, writing, teaching, and facilitating others' success. In the process, I have connected with my own source of joy.

Our time on this planet is short, and work is one of the primary vehicles for expressing our true self. Most of us spend more time working than in any other activity in life—even more than sleeping. My hope is that this book gives you the tools to create joyful, abundant, and sustainable work that embodies love and compassion—for yourself and for the whole world.

CHAPTER 2   What Is Liberation-Based Livelihood?

To practice Right Livelihood, you have to find a way to earn your living without transgressing your ideals of love and compassion. The way you support yourself can be an expression of your deepest self, or it can be a source of suffering for you and others. Our vocation can nourish our understanding and compassion, or erode them. We should be awake to the consequences, far and near, of the way we earn our living.

—Thich Nhat Hanh

The essence of Buddhism, as I understand it, is about freedom from suffering. The word "liberation" turns up over and over in Buddhist texts, but you don't have to be a Buddhist to want to be free. If you drill down deep into your own life, you'll begin to see how many of your choices are driven by a desire to free yourself from suffering.

The problem is that our attempts to end our pain can often lead us into more suffering. Not that we intend it that way! Without some kind of contemplative practice and the insights that come from it, it's easy to engage in not-so-helpful strategies like avoidance or addictive behaviors that may offer some short-term relief but actually perpetuate our unhappiness.

Most of us spend the majority of our time each week engaged in our work, and we give it a large portion of our vital energy. According to a 2016 survey from the Harvard School of Public Health, nearly half of working adults in the United States say that their current job affects their physical health, but only twenty-eight percent of those believe that the effect is a good one. People with disabilities, and in dangerous or low-paying jobs, are most likely to say their jobs have a negative impact on their stress levels, eating habits, and sleeping patterns. [3]

When we're unhappy in a job, that suffering permeates every aspect of our life. Conversely, when we're doing work that we love, it has a profoundly positive impact on the rest of our life (and the people around us).

When I reflect on my work history over these past decades, I can clearly see how some jobs brought me joy while others I suffered through—sometimes a little and sometimes a great deal. (This is an exploration you'll undertake when you do the "Mining for Gold" exercise in chapter 4.) Before I had a mindfulness practice, my tendency was to escape the dissatisfaction I felt in one job by jumping into another without giving much thought to what was going on inside me. Not surprisingly, I often ended up feeling equally miserable in the next job. It might take a month, it might take a year, but I'd find myself in the same predicament. Worse yet, I couldn't understand why.

The attempts I made to figure out this dilemma through things like career counseling and aptitude tests were of limited help because they only tapped into one layer of my personality.

Mindful awareness has helped me to understand that real change takes place primarily at the level of our mind-set and beliefs. We may try modifying external conditions only to discover that nothing has truly changed, as I learned from all my job-hopping. *Freedom is an inside job*: that's the fundamental principle of this book.

At the same time, it's important to recognize that there are unhealthy, even dangerous work situations that no amount of mindful reflection will change. When this is the case, it's entirely appropriate to call for reforms, and if you're the one working in that situation, to get yourself out of it as soon as possible. More on that in chapter 11, "Navigate the Three Pathways to Freedom."

The Buddha taught about Right Livelihood as one segment of the Eightfold Path. Right Livelihood, in this context, is a way to earn a living in which you don't harm others or yourself. Traditional teachings on Right Livelihood were fairly simple and focused on avoiding work that had harmful consequences for the worker as well as those who purchased his or her product or service.

The times we now live in are different from and often more complex than when the Buddha lived and taught more than two thousand years ago. For example, particularly in Western cultures, our sense of individuation is highly developed, for better or worse. And the speed and technology with which we work and live has exponentially increased. Work has become an extension of our identity and a primary way to express who we are.

Our global economy is also very different from the more village-based economies that existed during the Buddha's time. There were certainly some transnational trade routes like the Silk Road, but for the most part transactions happened on a very local level. In today's interconnected and digital economy, it's almost impossible to find a job or industry that, even if on its own is harmless, is not connected to another that is destructive in some way—environmentally, economically, and socially.

Finally, we've inherited beliefs about work that have been shaped by institutions and structures such as capitalism and patriarchy, often without our awareness. In the United States, the Protestant work ethic underlies many of our assumptions around work: we live to work instead of working to live. Beliefs like "time is money" can lead us to override the intelligence of our bodies and hearts, to not listen when they quietly (or loudly) say to us, "Enough!" When we accept, without question, these kinds of beliefs and assumptions, we limit our imagination about more nourishing possibilities for work.

All these factors, combined with my own personal experience, inspired me to look for updates to this teaching on Right Livelihood—think of it as "Right Livelihood 2.0"—and create the concept of Liberation-Based Livelihood. In addition to not causing harm to yourself or another, this is livelihood that is an expression of your Core Intention, work that you can fall in love with and that no longer feels like "work": work that matters.

Freedom is at the heart of this definition—freedom from limiting beliefs about what you're capable of and what work can look like, and freedom to fully express your Core Intention through your work. The late Anita Roddick, founder of the Body Shop and a dedicated human rights and environmental activist, described the spirit of a Liberation-Based Livelihood beautifully: "I have always found that my view of success has been iconoclastic: success to me is not about money or status or fame, it's about finding a livelihood that brings me joy and self-sufficiency and a sense of contributing to the world."[4]

Another simple way to describe this way of working comes from Leslie Rinchen-Wongmo, who we'll get to know more in chapter 4. For Leslie, a Liberation-Based Livelihood is present when "the things that I say I love and value and are important to me actually show up in what I do each day."

When I use the word "livelihood," please note that it's a placeholder for an entire constellation of work options. Some of these include:

full-time job • part-time job • job sharing
starting your own business or organization
contract work • paid internship • volunteer work
working in exchange for room, board, and stipend at a spiritual
center or work trade • a combination of any of the above

We'll explore these and other options in chapter 11.

For now, I invite you to consider that your livelihood is bigger than a job title. It's about your commitment to embody your Core Intention through the activity of work, in whatever position you hold (or create for yourself). When you start thinking about work like this, you'll stop trying to box yourself into a way-too-narrow job description. Instead, you focus on this commitment and begin to see innovative ways for your work to take form. You'll have a chance to articulate your own commitment when you create your Personal Mission Statement in chapter 10.

One of the most important things you'll take away from this book is the ability to radically redefine what "work" means, so you can be more creative about how it looks for you. Perhaps my own journey can serve to illustrate how this functions in real life.

As I mentioned when I shared my story in chapter 1, I picked my first career as a mental health professional because of my desire to help others. Eventually I realized that my choice to enter that field was driven by some codependency and that I overidentified as a "helper." Over the years as I've gotten to know my personality better and work through some of those issues, I've discovered that a genuine wish to be of service is still at the core of who I am—but I've been able to do it from a more wholesome place. What's also true is that I find a great deal of nourishment in Buddhist teachings and practice. When I had the opportunity to enroll in the Upaya Zen Center Buddhist Chaplaincy Training Program in 2010—which culminated in receiving ordination as a lay minister and chaplain—I saw it as a chance to deepen my understanding of both those streams: service and Buddhism. The essential skill of a chaplain, as I've come to understand it, is to accompany people through suffering in a way that empowers them to find their own source of strength and meaning.

While I occasionally offer spiritual mentoring, officiate weddings, and give Dharma talks (the Buddhist version of a sermon), my everyday occupation isn't directly related to chaplaincy or ministry. Instead, the training has given me another way to express my Core Intention: helping people to make discoveries and connections. For me, this means helping people to discover the resilience and spark that is deep inside of them, and supporting them to connect with others who will value them for who they truly are.

Even though I don't work as a professional chaplain in a setting such as a hospital, I bring those chaplaincy skills into every aspect of my livelihood, whether I'm guiding an organization through a marketing strategy or coaching an individual through a career transition. Sometimes I think of myself as a stealth chaplain.

In a Liberation-Based Livelihood, you are consciously and consistently connecting your Core Intention to your work, whatever your work may be. You learn how to be flexible and fluid with how you define your livelihood, and this allows you to creatively respond to ever-shifting circumstances.

One of the obstacles to realizing Liberation-Based Livelihood is that we tend to believe our own "press release." We can get attached to a professional identity that gives us a degree of security, financially and psychologically—but it can also confine and limit us.

We might think and say, "I'm a teacher." This can be a source of legitimate pride and we spend years building our knowledge and skills in our chosen profession. We attend conferences, publish articles in professional journals, get certifications and licenses, and so on. At the same time, this kind of identification can cut us off from what might be a deeper calling, a more whole and authentic version of ourselves. This is what was happening as I got further into my career as a mental health professional. Sometimes when we overidentify with a role it can also build walls that separate us from others.

Watch what happens when you shift from nouns to verbs. Rather than getting attached to being a "teacher," put the emphasis on "teaching." You may notice that you love to teach but that your teaching could take a different form than having a job title as a "teacher." Your teaching may happen outside a typical educational setting. Ram Dass often says, "Identify with your soul, not your role." What a great way to say it. You may want to sit with the following question: How much am I identifying with a job title rather than what I intuitively know is my work to share with the world?

The road to a Liberation-Based Livelihood is not finite. It doesn't come to an end when you accept a certain job or decide to follow a profession—it evolves as you do. Your path will become more conscious and more intentional as you go through the processes outlined in this book. As you integrate these concepts into your life, you will discover that you are no longer stumbling blindly from one job to another without a sense of cohesion or meaning or, worse yet, stuck in a workplace that is in opposition to your values. This book will show you how to create a career path that is deeply aligned with your Core Intention and discover work options that are responsive to the realities of your life.

THE THREE PATHWAYS TO LIBERATION-BASED LIVELIHOOD

From my perspective, there are three pathways to a Liberation-Based Livelihood:

1. Plan Your Exit Strategy
2. Love the Job You've Got
3. Create Work That You Love

We'll explore each in greater detail in chapter 11, "Navigate the Three Pathways to Freedom," but here's an overview of the different routes to begin thinking about. As you read them, consider where you are at right now in your journey and where you are feeling called to go.

1. YOU MAY NEED TO LEAVE YOUR CURRENT JOB TO BE IN ALIGNMENT WITH YOUR HEART

Traditional Buddhist teachings are quite specific about what does *not* fall into Right Livelihood. The five professions designated as harmful back in the days of the Buddha were, "Business in weapons, business in human beings [slave trade], business in meat, business in intoxicants, and business in poison" (Vanijja Sutta AN 5.177).

If you find yourself in an occupation that directly contradicts your values, you'll probably need to get out as quickly as you can (taking into account your financial needs). There is no minor adjustment that can resolve that dissonance with your integrity. From there you can move into either the second or third pathways.

2. YOU CAN CHANGE YOUR ATTITUDE TOWARD YOUR CURRENT JOB

You can bring more awareness of your Core Intention and your Personal Mission Statement to your current job. That's really all it takes—in that moment, as you reimagine your relationship with your employment through the lens of what is most valuable to you, you are embodying a Liberation-Based Livelihood. When you do this, your work will feel quite different, and even the most mundane job can be gratifying. It's a bit like being with a life partner for many years and thinking you know everything about them, and then realizing it's possible to see them in a new way and fall in love all over again.

You can support this internal realignment by taking concrete actions as well, such as identifying and then requesting changes to your working conditions that better support your happiness. We'll explore specific ways to do this in chapter 11.

3. YOU MAY WANT (OR NEED) TO CREATE YOUR OWN WORK ENVIRONMENT

When you try to fit yourself into job descriptions that aren't right for you, when you spend months on job searches that bear no fruit, you may be missing an opportunity right in front of you to create your own work reality. This could mean starting your own business, or working for others in combination with running your own business, or something else. The possibilities are in fact limitless.

Creating your own work is not for everyone. Robert Safian of *Fast Company* magazine coined the term "Generation Flux" to describe people who are comfortable with risk and change. This is not an age-based demographic, so you don't have to worry that you're too old (or too young). Safian writes, "To thrive in this climate requires a whole new approach.... What defines GenFlux is a mind-set that embraces instability, that tolerates—and even enjoys—recalibrating careers, business models, and assumptions."[5]

If you're the kind of person who has the capacity to embrace change, this may be the path for you. (That's one of the capacities that you will strengthen as you work through the process in this book, particularly in Key 4, "Make Friends with Uncertainty.") You might feel a little timid, but inwardly you believe you could thrive if you give yourself the opportunity to take chances and create your own work environment. Throughout this book, you'll meet people who are creating their own work and can serve as inspiration for you.

This is the path I've been following myself over the past decade. There's a learning curve involved, and income fluctuations can sometimes be a bit too thrilling for my taste, but I can guarantee you it's never boring!

CHAPTER 3   Three Building Blocks of Transformation

True transformation occurs only when we can look at ourselves
squarely and face our attachments and inner demons, free from the
buzz of commercial distraction and false social realities. We have
to retreat into our own cocoons and come face-to-face with who
we are. We have to turn toward our own inner darkness. For only
by abandoning its attachments and facing the darkness does the
caterpillar's body begin to spread out and its light, beautiful wings
begin to form.

—Julia Butterfly Hill

Transformation sounds wonderful and blissful, doesn't it? We imagine what we want to change or create in our lives and bingo! There it is. If only…

In reality, transformation is a messy process that requires us to unlearn old patterns before we can move into a new way of being. We often have to take two steps backward (or more) before we take a step forward. Anytime we are shifting long-held beliefs and habits, we are bound to run into discomfort. Along the way we will undoubtedly encounter our own resistance to change, which comes in every color of the rainbow.

As you dig into the process presented in this book, you may notice yourself taking numerous detours. You might put off reading the next chapter. You may get lost for hours on Facebook rather than doing one of the exercises. You may suddenly decide to give your house the most thorough cleaning ever. You may feel tempted to give up on the whole thing and settle for what you've got. Maybe your current employment situation is just fine…it pays the bills, right? And how much happiness can we expect from a job, anyway?

Whatever your favorite kind of resistance is, it is likely to go into full bloom as you start making changes to your livelihood because this is an area that is linked with survival (our job is what pays our bills) as well as identity (our job is how we define ourselves). As a matter of fact, the more resistance you encounter, the more likely that you're hitting pay dirt in your transformational process.

The three building blocks in this chapter will support you to overcome this resistance and discover new ways of thinking about survival and identity. I encourage you to return to them over and over as you work through the exercises in the rest of this book. You'll also find them helpful if you want to transform other aspects of your life, including physical well-being, the quality of your relationships, and more.

As you work with each of these building blocks, you may notice that it's similar to the process of working out a muscle. When you go to the gym and focus on developing strength in your thighs, for example, at the beginning it might feel strange as you exert muscles that you haven't used much. You'll likely feel a bit sore the next day! But, over time, you'll notice that you've increased the capacity of that muscle. In the same way, it will feel more natural to do these exercises as you integrate these qualities into your life.

1. RETURNING TO THIS VERY MOMENT

The "muscle" you're developing: self-awareness

During one period of my life, I had an hour-long commute to a job in San Francisco. On plenty of mornings, I'd pull into the office parking lot and realize I had no idea how I got there. I would remember stepping into my car at home, but then I was on a kind of autopilot for the next fifty minutes until I arrived at my destination. I had some blurry impressions of traffic and hills, but mostly my awareness was somewhere else entirely. And I couldn't tell you where that was! It was rather terrifying to realize this, but I have a feeling that being so checked out we don't remember how we got to work is a common experience for many of us. Our everyday habits become so ingrained from our routines as to propel us through our days without much awareness on our parts. This is called "habit energy."

We can live our lives that way too, going through the motions of our jobs, our relationships, and then "waking up" weeks, months, sometimes years later, and wonder how we ended up where we are.

Mindfulness is an invitation to change that pattern and to become aware of where we are and how we got here. Mindfulness gives us a chance to listen to the wisdom of our hearts, to notice with more clarity where we get in our own way, and to shift from reacting out of habit to responding from our intentions.

The practice of mindfulness is one of the most powerful reset buttons we have. When we learn how to slow down internally, we begin to see our habitual reactive patterns. We start to understand how fear, even on subtle levels, may dictate our choices around our work.

Katya Lesher, an artist who took the online version of Fall in Love with Your Work, describes the impact that sitting meditation has on her life:

> *My practice helps me every single day, even when I feel like a failure or feel totally lost. I know that comes from my "monkey mind," not from the core of me. When I start believing what my mind is telling me, I can go down a hole that is not very healthy or helpful. My practice is not just about sitting on the cushion— any given moment can be a practice.*

If you already have a mindfulness or contemplative practice, consider doubling your commitment to it during the time you move through the process of this book. I mean that quite literally. If you currently do sitting meditation or yoga three times a week for ten minutes a day, increase that to six times a week for twenty minutes a day, if you can. That may not always be possible, but give it your best shot. I can testify from my own experience and from watching the people who have gone through Fall in Love with Your Work that the deeper the ground of your practice, the more you will get out of this process.

Here's something that is a revelation for most people: There are many different kinds of mindfulness practice. The one we most often think of is sitting meditation, which can present a stumbling block if you don't think you're good at it.

When I was the research director for the Center for Contemplative Mind in Society from 2002 to 2004, I had the wonderful opportunity to listen to more than eighty leaders talk about how they brought contemplative practice into settings such as healthcare, business, and education. As I analyzed the transcripts of these interviews, I created the "Tree of Contemplative Practices" as a visual way to convey the diverse forms of practice the interviewees were describing.

The Tree has helped many people to find a practice that best suits their personality and temperament. Perhaps it will help you consider how to make practice the foundation of your explorations throughout this book.

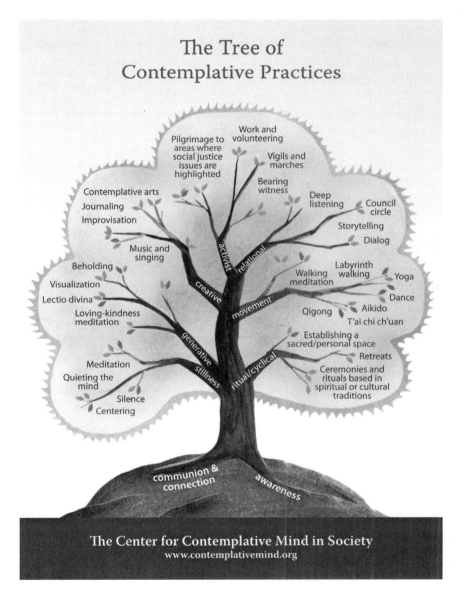

This is my personal definition of "practice": an activity that you do on a regular basis (ideally each day) that helps you to cultivate a sense of self-awareness, joy, equanimity, resilience, and compassion for yourself and others. The Tree, along with this expansive definition, can increase your possibilities for integrating a practice into your life.

For Lauren Ayer, a Fall in Love with Your Work graduate, practice took the form of participating in a 365-day photo challenge. She started it before a difficult relationship breakup and continued it throughout that experience and beyond:

> *I ended up doing the photo challenge for 444 days. All I had were pictures of flowers and nature and the river. I realized that in the middle of one of the darkest periods of my life, every day I found beauty. Clearly that was what I needed most to get through it. … I had no idea what amazing medicine I was performing on myself without knowing it.*

Another course graduate, Leslie Rinchen-Wongmo, a textile artist and teacher with a background in Tibetan Buddhist practice, spoke about how her practice extends off the meditation cushion and provides a framework for her work and life:

> *My practice is so interwoven with my life. In some ways I'm a very undisciplined practitioner. My sitting practice is sometimes very steady and other times not so much. Even though my practice is erratic in some ways, it's always the foundation of my life. It creates a container for every interaction that I have.*
>
> *My practice gives me a standard with which I can look at every interaction in my life and ask whether it is contributing to what my deepest values are, whether it's opening my heart, and whether I'm living in integrity and finding ways to be kind. My practice is a lot about understanding—looking at the world and myself and recognizing that things are not necessarily how I see them.*

A GUIDE TO SITTING MEDITATION

While there are many forms of contemplative practice and I encourage you to explore what practice looks like for you, sitting meditation is a very simple and powerful way to cultivate mindfulness and self-awareness. If meditation is new to you or if you need a refresher, here are the instructions I like to offer:

1. Create Space and Time for Your Practice

Space: Find a quiet space in your home and designate it as your meditation space. This doesn't have to be a big area, but it does help if this is the only activity you do in it. Trying to meditate at your work desk is generally not a good idea. (You may find that you enjoy taking mindful breaks from your work, but that is not the same as the consistent and longer period of meditation described here.)

You may want to create a simple altar with objects that have special meaning for you—for example, pictures of loved ones and people who inspire you, or stones from a place in nature that nourishes you.

Set up a meditation cushion or chair in this space, whatever works best for you. We'll look more at posture in a minute.

Time: It helps to meditate at the same time each day so that you can establish your practice as a habit. Consider your daily routine and decide on a time that will work best for you. Some spiritual traditions consider the hour before sunrise to be the most auspicious time for meditation. That's a bit too early for me, but I find that it works best to meditate first thing in the morning before I do anything else. The longer I put it off, the easier it becomes to make excuses about not having time.

Choose an amount of time for your meditation period. If you are just beginning, I suggest sitting a minimum of five minutes each day. You can gradually increase from there. I find that a twenty-five-minute sitting period is optimal for me; other people like to sit in thirty-five- or forty-five-minute periods. With experimentation you will discover what is right for you.

It's helpful to set a timer so that you can release yourself from the need to check a clock every so often. There are some fancy, expensive meditation timers (like the Enso), or you can use your phone (don't forget to turn the ringer off!), or even a simple kitchen timer.

Meditation is most effective when you practice it on a consistent basis, ideally every day at the same time. It's better to meditate for a short period of time each day rather than skipping days and then sitting longer amounts of time to make up for it. Aim for consistency.

2. Find the Posture That Works for You

If you don't have physical limitations, it's

SEIZA

usually best to sit on a meditation cushion (sometimes called a *zafu*) on the floor rather than on a chair. If you're sitting on a cushion, you have a couple of choices. One is to sit on your knees (sometimes called *seiza* position), either using a meditation bench or putting your cushion in a vertical position.

LOTUS   HALF LOTUS

The other choices are to sit cross-legged in a **full lotus or half lotus position**. In full lotus, both feet are placed near the top of your thighs. In half lotus, one foot is placed on the top of your thigh while the other touches the ground.

If you are new to meditation, these positions, particularly the full lotus, can be more challenging to hold for a long period of time. You may want to start out sitting in a chair or in the kneeling position and ease your way into the cross-legged positions.

In the kind of sitting meditation I do, *zazen*, it's important to hold your body as still as possible throughout the meditation period and not react if you have an unpleasant sensation such as an itch or an ache. In other meditation traditions, being still is not as critical. However you do it, it's good to practice staying with a sensation for as long as possible before you change your body posture.

This may seem difficult at first when you experience aches or pains, but these sensations can become objects of your meditation, and you can investigate them more thoroughly. If you feel a pain in your leg, for example, notice the length and quality of the ache, and notice how it changes over the course of your observation of it. There is a life lesson here: meditation can help us cultivate more resilience in the face of difficult circumstances (more on that when we get to the second building block, "Leveraging Adversity").

3. Start by Paying Attention to Your Body and Breath

People often have the idea that meditation is all about the mind, but actually it's a very physical experience. Breath and body go together in this practice, though in our daily life we may not often experience them in an integrated way. Meditation is all about bringing dualities into oneness. This is a chance to work with your breath and connect it back to your body.

As you begin your sitting meditation, take time to become aware of what's going on in your body. What sensations are you experiencing? You might notice that you feel discomfort in your back, or stiffness in your knees. You may also notice that you feel just fine, that your body is relaxed. Whatever comes up for you, simply become aware of the sensations without any judgment. It can be helpful to label these sensations as "pleasant," "unpleasant," or "neutral" as a way of bypassing any stories you may get lost in about what's happening in your body.

This is perhaps the most important point of meditation practice: You don't need to change anything, you simply need to notice. This first step of the practice is to raise your awareness of what is happening on a physical level. In this way, you begin to reconnect with your body.

Pay attention to your posture, especially your spine. Visualize a thread going from the base of your vertebrae, where your buttocks make contact with the cushion or seat of your chair, all the way through your spine to the top of your head and beyond that to the sky. Breathe gently into this thread and allow that breath to help your backbone naturally come into alignment, without too much effort.

Now, in the same way that you paid attention to your body, turn your attention to your breathing. Notice the quality of your breathing—is it shallow, deep, or something in between? Become aware of the sensation of taking in air through your nostrils, and follow the path of the breath as it makes its way down into your lungs. Again—there is no need to change anything about your breathing, simply become more deeply aware of the act of breathing (and what a gift it is).

4. Awareness of Thoughts and Emotions

Once you have centered yourself in your body and breath, from that place of stability you can turn your attention to thoughts and emotions that you may be experiencing. You may want to name them as they arise; for example: "Joy," or "Worry," or "Fear," or "Contentment." The idea here is to simply take note of them, once again without judgment. And without creating a story around them.

For example, if you notice that you feel angry, become aware of what the energy of anger feels like as it makes its way through your body. Try to not attach an explanation or story as to why it is there or whom it is directed toward. "Anger" is simply a sensation just like the ones that you have begun to notice in your body and breath.

Here's a friendly warning: meditation can churn up a lot of sludge from your unconsciousness. That is really the whole point—to bring those less conscious aspects of ourselves into the light of awareness. This sludge might come in the form of a torrent of thoughts, perhaps not so pleasant:

- "How will I ever find a job that makes me happy?"
- "I can't stand my landlord!"
- "Did I remember to turn the iron off before I left?"

... and so forth.

Once you have created more internal space through your meditation practice you may also start feeling things that you have long suppressed. Or if you are going through a particularly difficult situation in your workplace, meditation may open a floodgate of emotions. All of this is okay ... the practice is to simply learn how to witness these thoughts and feelings without getting swept away by them.

Again, there is an important life lesson here. This practice is teaching us how to be present to the conditions of our life without feeling overwhelmed by them. We are learning how to find a place of equanimity within, a sense of balance, even if the outer circumstances of our life are in turmoil.

As a thought arises in your mind, see if you can get into the habit of simply noting it without entertaining it. (That's a funny expression, isn't it? "Let me entertain that thought.")

One way to do this is the practice of labeling your thoughts. You might notice that you tend to dwell on things in your past that you wish you had done differently. When these kinds of thoughts arise for me, I gently say to myself, "Replaying," because what I am doing is replaying a past scene in my life, ad nauseam, just like a bad movie. You may find that you are planning for a future encounter or event. When this happens to me, I say, "Rehearsing."

You can use the same technique with emotions. You might discover that you're feeling sadness, or anger, or even joy. If you watch carefully, you begin to realize that all of these feelings will rise up and pass away. In the very moment that you have noticed the thought or feeling, you have just had an experience of awareness. Buddhist teacher Sharon Salzberg calls this "the magic moment." This is exactly when you get to practice being present to yourself, over and over and over.

Your body and breath can serve as your anchors. Often during my meditation period I'll say to myself: "Come back home to my body; come back home to my breath." This helps me return attention to my body and breath, and the stability and grounding that are present there. You can try this phrase or experiment with another that helps you to return to your practice.

2. LEVERAGING ADVERSITY

The muscle you're developing: resilience

As you move through the exercises in this book and build your self-awareness muscle through mindfulness practice, watch how you respond to challenging situations. These challenges might come to you externally, like a toxic boss, or internally, like your own tendency toward depression or negativity. The idea behind "Leveraging Adversity" is that you're able to take the source of a challenge and conjure up the energy to shift it into something positive—or at least neutral. Think of the old but trusty saying, "turning lemons into lemonade." Another useful metaphor is aikido, the Japanese martial art. Rather than focusing on attacking the opponent, students of aikido practice redirecting the momentum of their opponent in order to gain control of them. This is what you're doing when you leverage adversity.

We hear a lot about PTSD, post-traumatic stress disorder. A growing body of knowledge indicates that there is also such a thing as post-traumatic growth. Think of Malala Yousafzai, the young Pakistani woman who was shot in the shoulder, neck, and head by a Taliban gunman in 2012. This devastating attack could have killed Malala, or at the least put an end to her passion for advocating for human rights. Not only did she physically recover, she became even more committed to this cause. Malala said, "The terrorists thought they would change my aims and stop my ambitions, but nothing changed in my life except this: weakness, fear, and hopelessness died. Strength, power, and courage were born."

This is what is possible when you learn how to leverage adversity and develop resilience. Imagine if you could take your negative and even traumatic past work experiences and turn them into the foundation of work that truly matters to you. We'll get a chance to do that when you go through the Mining for Gold exercise in Key 1, Become Intimate with Your Core Intention. First, though, let's look at these simple but powerful practices to help you work out your resilience muscle.

GRATITUDE

Gratitude is a very powerful alchemical force, which we have direct access to in our everyday lives. By shifting our attention from what we think we lack to what we actually have, we create new possibilities. Benedictine monk Brother David Steindl-Rast has said, "In daily life we must see that it is not happiness that makes us grateful, but grateful-ness that makes us happy."

You can bring this practice of gratitude to each step of the process outlined in this book. For example, when you're doing the Mining for Gold exercise (on page 67), you may start to feel despair about a painful work-related memory. If that happens, practice shifting your focus to what you appreciated about that experience. It might be as simple as, "That job helped me realize that I *never* want to work in the health care system again." Gratitude practice helps you recognize that you received a gift of discernment from that difficult experience.

Another way to cultivate gratitude is to keep a journal to document your appreciation. Set aside time each week to reflect on everything that has been a gift for you during the previous seven days. Nothing is too big or too small to include in your list: a phone conversation with a friend, a clerk at a store who took time to give you extra help, the sound of your daughter's laughter, your persistence in going to the gym, whatever it is for you. All the things that are so easy to overlook in the course of a busy life are the perfect things to include on your list.

STOP THE SPIN

"Spin doctors" are public relations folks who specialize in taking infor-mation and "spinning" it in ways meant to influence and manipulate others. We often do the same thing to ourselves without realizing it.

There is what actually happens—and then there is the story we tell ourselves about what happens. In between the two is the difference between peace and suffering. For example, let's say you've been laid off from your job. The outcome of this event can go in many directions. It could be a difficult experience, and it also has the potential to benefit you. Step back from the situation and look at its most basic level: It's simply an event that occurred. Then notice what you have layered onto that event. Do you start telling yourself that you'll be unemployable for the rest of your life and living on the streets within a week, and work yourself into a panic? Or perhaps your tendency is to move in the other direction. You throw on your rose-colored glasses, tell yourself everything is fine, and refuse to deal with issues that are related to the layoff. Notice whatever your default story is.

This is where basic mindfulness practice can be a huge support. See if you can stay with your initial experience of an event and gently stop yourself when you notice that you're going beyond that with an interpretation about it. Emotions of sadness, grief, and anger are all absolutely natural and it's essential for us to feel them in response to difficult situations. We get into trouble when we attach unhelpful narratives to those emotions, which then prevent us from seeing things clearly and taking productive action.

3. STAYING THE COURSE

The muscle you're developing: persistence

You're cultivating a mindfulness practice that gives you a ground of self-awareness. You've started to face adversity in a new way so that you can turn challenges into opportunities.

There is one more "muscle" that will help you make the most of this process—persistence. The Latin root of the word means "to stand through, steadfast." Persisting is about standing strong no matter what. To persist means to continue even when you feel you've reached your limit. You may encounter that point in the midst of adversity, or it may also come from simple exhaustion, boredom, or impatience.

The process of transformation has dramatic points and peak experiences for sure. But it's also a matter of translating those peak moments into an ongoing, consistent practice. This is where "Staying the Course" becomes so important.

Anytime you make an effort to shift something big in your life, be ready for backward steps and disappointments. This is inevitable. An essential component of transformation is that we need to bump up against what has kept us in our current state—this bumping up can sometimes feel rough and we may want to bail out.

Here are three practices to support you in building your persistence muscle: (1) stay connected to your "why," (2) give yourself a structure, and (3) find an accountability buddy.

1. Stay Connected to Your "Why"

The more you remember your intention for doing a task, the more likely you'll stick with it when the going gets tough or tedious.

Before moving into the next chapter and working with the first Key to Liberation-Based Livelihood, I invite you to sit with the following questions and allow some time to journal on them. If you're more of a visual person, you may wish to create a collage of photos or drawings in response to these questions:

- What is it costing me in terms of my peace of mind to stay in my current work situation and not make any changes?
- What is it costing me in terms of emotional well-being?
- What is it costing me in terms of my physical health?
- What would it feel like if every morning I had work to do that is inspiring and invigorating?
- How would my life be different if my work truly mattered and made a real contribution to the lives of others?

As you reflect on these questions, you may notice an intention becomes clear, a reason why it's important for you to persist in this quest to create a Liberation-Based Livelihood. My intention sounded like this: "I realize that my current job is literally making me sick. I am yearning to find a way to share my gifts with the world through my work. So my intention is to stay on this path until I find or create a nourishing work situation where my greatest gifts can come shining through."

Write your intention on a piece of paper and place it somewhere where you'll see it every day and can be reminded why you are doing this. When you hit those inevitable rough patches and feel tempted to quit, take a moment to reconnect with this intention.

2. Give Yourself a Structure

Create a schedule for going through the chapters and exercises in this book. Even an informal one is fine; the point is to give yourself some structure to support you to "stay the course." Perhaps you will commit to read one chapter a week and do the exercises in it, or maybe one chapter a month—whatever feels doable in the scope of your life. This is about pacing yourself and drawing on the power of rhythm and rituals to keep your momentum.

In the book *The Power of Full Engagement*, authors Tony Schwartz and James Loehr took a look at the factors that separate high-performing athletes from average ones. They found that high performers have a unique ritual that helps them to make a clean break between activities, allowing them to quickly drop into a state of relaxation and then return to the task with renewed awareness. In contrast, average athletes just keep pounding away with no such demarcation between "on" states and relaxation. In the process, they deplete their physical strength and mental awareness. Think of a star tennis player like Serena Williams and notice how she religiously bounces the ball five times before her first serve. That's her ritual and that's what helps her to reset her focus.

What kinds of rituals can you create to make a distinction between your time to focus on the process in this book and your time to relax? For example, you might use a special notebook dedicated to doing the exercises in this book. That's the only thing you use it for, and every time you bring it out to work on this process, do so with some kind of fanfare!

Another aspect of ritual is celebration. Make sure to celebrate your accomplishments as you move through this book, even the small ones. Every time that you complete a chapter and the exercises in it, schedule a treat for yourself. Maybe it's a bubble bath, or time with a friend, or cappuccino at your favorite coffee shop. Whatever works for you, give yourself time and space to mark your successes.

3. Find an Accountability Buddy

Healthy peer pressure can be a wonderful thing! You don't have to do this process alone. Think of a friend who shares your desire to find work that they love and ask if they want to join as you go through the exercises in this book. The two of you can get together every month, every week, or whatever timing you agree on to compare notes and cheer each other on. As you will learn in Key 6, surrounding yourself with a circle of friends who support your aspiration to have a Liberation-Based Livelihood is essential to actualizing it.

You can also find a supportive learning community connected to this book at this website: maiaduerr.com/work-that-matters.

PART II
The 6 Keys to Liberation-Based Livelihood

CHAPTER 4   Key 1: Become Intimate with Your Core Intention

There is a vitality, a life force, an energy, a quickening that is translated through you into action, and because there is only one of you in all time, this expression is unique. And if you block it, it will never exist through any other medium and it will be lost.... You have to keep yourself open and aware to the urges that motivate you. Keep the channel open.

—Martha Graham

The closer you get to understanding your "why," the more you'll arrive at a place where work feels like a natural expression of the gifts that you are here to offer. You'll find it's something you want to do nearly all the time, not just in the context of a nine-to-five day. As wisdom-teacher-disguised-as-country-singer Dolly Parton says, "Find out who you are and do it on purpose!"

As I shared in chapter 1, I've had dozens of jobs and at least five careers. My search for "true love" in the form of work has sometimes felt like going through a series of one-night stands, with momentary fulfillment but an overall sense of dissatisfaction and confusion.

As my career odyssey unfolded and as my meditation practice deepened, I gradually became more aware of what I cared about and how I could contribute to the things I cared about in my own unique way. My friend, Zen Buddhist teacher Alan Senauke, says it this way: "We are responsible for the world and to the world we live in. A gift has been given to us to share with everyone." I've come to understand this gift as my Core Intention.

Your Core Intention is your "why"—the urge that motivates you, as Martha Graham describes it, your reason for being on the planet. It lives inside you at an emotional level and it's where you feel the most alive to yourself and to the world around you.

When you first encounter it in a genuine way, your Core Intention may not make a lot of sense to anyone, including yourself. It may not fit into other people's preconceived ideas about what you should be doing or even your own ideas about what you should do. Understanding your Core Intention is essential to creating a Liberation-Based Livelihood. In fact, it can't happen without it.

WHAT'S YOUR RELATIONSHIP WITH THIS KEY?

Ask yourself the following questions to assess your current relationship with this key:

- How inspired do I feel by my current job/work situation?
- How much does my current job/work situation give me a sense of meaning and purpose?
- How much does my current job feel in conflict with my deepest values?
- How often do I wake up in the morning and wonder why I am going to work?

In the early days of teaching this course, this Key was originally called "Get Clear on Your Core Intention." However, as I reflected on my own journey and heard others' stories, I realized there isn't an end point at which to say, "Oh, that's it! Now I know my Core Intention and it's not going to change." Rather, like any meaningful relationship, this process of understanding your Core Intention will change and deepen over time. The name for this Key evolved into, "Become Intimate with Your Core Intention," in acknowledgment that there is always something wonderfully new to discover.

To me, intimacy means a familiarity that comes about when we are willing to be completely honest with ourselves, augmented with a healthy dose of radical self-acceptance. It's kind of like coming out of the shower and standing in front of the mirror, looking at your naked body, noticing that flabby spot by your tummy or that scar on your leg, and being completely okay with all of it. The process that unfolds in this chapter will take you on a tour of your inner world as well as to places in your past that are related to your work, and not all of them will be easy to look at. This is not a journey for the fainthearted! But as you make your way through the explorations here, you'll become more intimate with the ingredients that come together to form your Core Intention.

While your Core Intention will begin to clarify as you go through this chapter and the rest of the book, like a vibrant love affair, the object of your love will keep on fascinating and surprising you as you discover more of its layers and dimensions.

The distinction between "intention" and "goal" is important. Intention comes from the heart and soul. A goal is an explicit manifestation of that intention. A Core Intention is also a bit different than your "purpose," though there is a connection between them. Jami Sieber, a musician, puts it well:

> Whenever someone shows me a book about getting in touch with your purpose in life, it scares me. When we are asked to get in touch with our purpose, I always felt that it had to be a plan, a goal, a "job." Now I understand it more in terms of an energy. What is it my heart is needing? Why is my spirit here? Why am I on this planet?

At this stage of the process, I encourage you to focus on your "why" more than the "what" or "how" of the equation. We'll tackle these later when you create your Personal Mission Statement in chapter 10. You can easily get sidetracked in trying to figure out the specifics of what you want do for work and miss out on this very essential first step. Creative quilter and writer Lauren, a graduate of Fall in Love with Your Work, shared her experience:

> When I took the course the first time, I was trying hard to focus on "what"—am I a quilter? Am I writer? The more I tried to nail that down, the more confused I got. Because I'd start to focus on one and I'd pine for the other one. Everything shifted when I realized that the important thing to focus on wasn't whether I was writing or quilting, it was why I was writing or quilting and what I was trying to say.

In this chapter, you'll explore your Core Intention from three different angles—what I call "Survive, Alive, and Thrive," for short. First you'll look at beliefs you've inherited about yourself and the concept of work that have helped you to navigate the world and survive, but may obstruct you from finding your deeper calling. Then you'll have a chance to explore what makes you feel most alive. Finally you'll reflect on past jobs that hold clues about the conditions you need to thrive. By the time you get to the end of this chapter, I hope you'll have a beginning version of your Core Intention, which will become a foundational piece of the mission statement that you'll create in chapter 10.

As you go through this process, you may realize that it's not possible to express your Core Intention in your current job. For example, your Core Intention may be to share wholehearted enthusiasm with people and to help them discover their own source of joy. If you're working in an environment that does not allow you to share that gift with others, you'll be forever frustrated. This is helpful information, and we'll look at practical strategies for what to do in this case when we get to chapter 11.

Or you may notice that your Core Intention is inherent in the work you now do, but you may be able to express it in a more aware and conscious way. In either case, the insights you gain through this process can help you make positive changes to align your work with your Core Intention.

KEY 1 PRACTICES
1. WHAT DID I LEARN TO SURVIVE?
The first step in making a big life transformation usually involves unlearning. We need to be able to see and acknowledge the false layers of "self" we've acquired over the years as we've done our best to navigate life and its many challenges. Only then can we gently release them and thus make space for our authentic self to shine through. Spiritual teacher Adyashanti describes this quite beautifully:

> *To study yourself does not mean to add more knowledge to your cluttered brain's ideas about yourself, but to remove all of the customary defining characteristics you usually associate self with: name, race, gender, occupation, social status, past, as well as all of the psychological judgments you make about yourself. When the self is stripped down to its essential core, all that can be said about it is: 'I am; I exist.' What then is the I that exists?* [6]

Throughout our lives, we've received a lot of messages about what we are supposed to be good at and care about, as well as what "work" should look and feel like. Some of these messages come from our families, some from our culture, and some from a combination of both. This conditioning is based on gender, ethnicity, economic class, and many other factors. It is usually accompanied by the message (spoken or unspoken): "That's just the way life is," which makes it difficult to recognize. These beliefs become so ingrained in us that we may take them to be unquestionable truths.

Consider that we eat with a fork and knife only because when we were growing up, that's what we saw everyone around us doing. We stop for red lights only because of a collective cultural agreement. There is nothing inherent in forks and knives or red lights that require us to respond to them as we do. But we have been so thoroughly conditioned in those actions that it seems like the only rational response.

These inherited beliefs and values may not line up with what is deeper in your heart. If you look closely, you may discover that you've based many of your decisions about work on ideas that belong to someone else. Often we don't even have a clue what it is that we truly love to do. We haven't yet asked ourselves the questions that could bring out our more authentic selves. Lyndon Marcotte, another Fall in Love with Your Work graduate, shared this:

> *If you had asked me about my passion when I was younger, I couldn't really answer that question. I could give some clichés, but I spent so many years being whatever people needed me to be. It wasn't until later in my life that I asked myself, "So, what kind of music do I like?" or "When I choose for myself what I do in my free time, what do I do?" It took years to figure out the answers to those questions.*

Through this process, Ann, another course graduate, discovered that most of her adult life had been motivated by a sense of duty. She said, "The act of looking up from that well-trodden path of 'doing what I should' and trying to see what brings me joy is like trying a new and difficult yoga pose! I feel like the answers I'm coming up with today aren't necessarily the final answer."

By uncovering the hidden scripts that we grew up with, we give ourselves many more choices about how to respond to a situation as well as how to create work that is truly meaningful to us. Gender is a very big source of these scripts and expectations. In many parts of the world, men (particularly heterosexual men) are conditioned to avoid any roles or situations in which they perceive themselves as "weak." This may lead them to rule out certain occupations such as nursing or teaching, even if they feel an affinity toward those vocations. This conditioning works in the other direction as well. In a 2014 study from the University of Exeter in the United Kingdom, researchers found that the excessively macho atmosphere of the Royal Marines was a deterrent to those who worried they might not be "man enough" to fit in.[7]

Women, on the other hand, are often conditioned to take on the "caring" narrative—a reason many of us organize our careers around responding to other people's needs and go into the helping professions. That's what I did for the first ten years of my working life until I realized something inside of me felt very out of balance.

Your impulse to care may be a genuine calling, but it's worthwhile to closely examine how fulfilling this path has actually been in your lived experience.

It's also possible that you grew up in a very progressive environment and took on the values around you. Again, the invitation is to consider how much they are actually *your* values, and where they might be imposing limitations on what you feel is possible in your life. Yael Raff Peskin, who now runs Kulanu, a year-round, outdoor early childhood program that she created on her country property in northern California, speaks about how her feminist background initially caused her to turn away from working with children:

> In 1974, I turned nineteen years old and began working at the Feminist Women's Health Center in Los Angeles. It was a time when growing numbers of women were breaking into what had been considered nontraditional roles for women: doctors, lawyers, judges, journeypeople, firefighters. It was a time of breaking down barriers, and honoring women's intellect and physical strength. We were giddy for each new accomplishment for womankind!
>
> Although it was a popular slogan of the day to say that it was a woman's choice whether or not (or when) to have children, there was still a prevalent feeling that being at home, raising children, was less important work than being out in the world breaking new ground. Honestly, I don't think I could have done the work I'm doing with children today before now. Forty years ago, even five years ago, the idea of being a preschool teacher did not seem to me to be the path of a radical feminist.

In the process of going through the exercises in this chapter and the rest of the book, you may discover that you've adapted to certain kinds of jobs and a way of working because that's what your family and society have expected from you. This unlearning process will help you identify some of these beliefs and assumptions so that you can make a conscious choice whether or not to continue allowing them to inform your life.

UNLEARNING EXPLORATION #1: SOCIAL CONDITIONING

Take time to read through the open-ended sentences below and complete them, being as honest with yourself as you can. Notice what comes up for you in the process of doing this. Even if you think you no longer hold a certain belief, make note of it. Could it still be at play in your life, in more subtle ways?

As with all the exercises in this book, please make sure to offer yourself a great deal of self-compassion. If you feel a negative judgment arising about some of the life and work choices you've made, you may want to remind yourself, "I realize that I have done the best I can, given my circumstances."

GENDER

As a young girl or someone raised as a girl, I learned that girls should …
    Some possibilities:

- take care of themselves
- take care of others
- be tough
- be kind
- be agreeable
- be nice
- be competitive
- be independent

As a young girl or someone raised as a girl, I learned that some jobs were out of the question for me, such as …

As a young boy or someone raised as a boy, I learned that boys should…
    Some possibilities:

- take care of themselves
- take care of others
- be tough
- be kind

- be agreeable
- be nice
- be competitive
- be independent

As a young boy or someone raised as a boy, I learned that some jobs were out of the question for me, such as ...

ETHNICITY

As a young person coming from [your ethnic background], some of the beliefs I inherited about work included ...

As a young person coming from [your ethnic background], I learned that some jobs were out of the question for me, such as ...

CLASS

As a young person coming from a [choose one that feels most appropriate to you] low-income/working-class/middle-class/upper-class family, some of the beliefs I inherited about work included ...

As a young person coming from a low-income/working-class/middle-class/upper-class family, I learned that some jobs were out of the question for me, such as ...

WHAT ELSE?

As you were growing up, what other conditions played a role in the way you view work? For example, did your religious upbringing convey certain teachings about work? Or perhaps you grew up differently abled with a hearing impairment, or a condition such as dyslexia. What messages did you receive from your family and others about work, in relationship to this condition?

As you review all your responses above, take a moment to do a basic mindfulness practice. Remember the sitting meditation practice back in chapter 3? This is a condensed version of that, one that you can do in less than a minute and yet can infuse you with a healthy dose of awareness. Take three deep breaths and check in with your body, heart, and mind. How do you feel?

How does it feel to know that you can choose a different way of understanding your reality?

UNLEARNING EXPLORATION #2: WHAT DOES WORK MEAN TO ME?

By accepting without question the assumptions and beliefs our culture has about work, we limit our imagination about how we relate to our work, and other more nourishing ways that work can take form. This exploration can help you become more aware of these assumptions—a first step toward questioning their validity.

Consider how many of the following phrases have played a part or even determined how you've made choices related to work—including the jobs you've chosen to apply for and the choices you made while in those jobs. Circle the ones that resonate the most strongly for you.

- Time is money.
- Being an adult means sucking it up and working even when I hate my job.
- I need to work really hard until I retire so I have enough in my retirement account.
- There's more security in working for someone else than working for myself.
- I have to mold myself to fit into the job description that is out there.
- Big gaps in my résumé make it harder for me to get a job.
- I really love to [fill in the blank] but I could never make money doing that.

What other beliefs have shaped your relationship to work?

As you look at each phrase you circled, take a moment to do a basic mindfulness practice. Take three deep breaths and check in with your body, heart, and mind. How do you feel?

How does it feel to know that you can choose a different way of understanding your reality?

2. WHAT MAKES ME FEEL ALIVE?

Leslie Rinchen-Wongmo is one of very few non-Tibetans creating silk appliqué *thangkas*, sacred textile artworks that support meditation practice. Through her Stitching Buddhas Virtual Apprentice Program, she teaches this craft to women around the globe, helping them connect the spiritual and creative threads in their own lives. In her words, she's on a "mission to connect." Leslie says:

I hope my work can be a contribution to the preservation and appreciation of Tibetan culture. My art comes out of and is integrally connected with a profound spiritual tradition. Each piece should function to bless and inspire those who commission it as well as all those who see it. The form itself is imbued with spirit and I try to work in such a way as to enhance that essence throughout my process and in each completed piece.

Yael Raff Peskin, the preschool director whom we met earlier, says:

I am grateful beyond measure for all of the love I received from my own parents, as a young child and into my adult years, and I feel a great responsibility to share that love with others. I value the long and winding journey I have taken through Jewish tradition, feminism, Zen mindfulness practice, Waldorf education, and being a parent to my own children. I feel incredibly blessed to be creating an environment where I can share so much of my experience in all of these realms; where the journey of my own life can play a role in nurturing and supporting others on their own journeys.

For Katya Lesher, it's clear:

I love to make art. After working in hospice for eight years and having very little energy to make art, I felt like my soul was dying. That experience showed me that it's crucial for me to be able to create. I also love to create space and environments for myself and others, to be able to help others in their process of healing using creative expression and contemplative practice. I help people discover the "pausing turtle" in them.

For Katya, the "pausing turtle" symbolizes the importance of slowing down, stopping, and paying attention—an essential element in the healing journey, from her perspective.

Lyndon Marcotte, now working as a hospice chaplain in Louisiana after an unsatisfying career in healthcare marketing, says:

Helping to end suffering in other people, whether that's mental, physical, or spiritual—that's when I feel most alive, useful, satisfied, not in the sense of being a doormat but genuinely making a difference. You can't put a price tag on that, in terms of the satisfaction I get.

Jami Sieber, a cellist who was deeply inspired on a journey to Thailand and time she spent with elephants, says:

> When people come to my concerts, I want them to feel the love I feel for them and for my music. I want them to feel the beauty of the elephant that inspired this song, or the beauty of the sky that brought another song. That's what I want to convey. I feel that our world is starved for beauty, and I feel that it's the gift I have to share.

Leslie, Yael, Eatya, Lyndon, and Jami are wonderful examples of what it looks like when you've found your Core Intention. Each of them feels a profound sense of purpose, and each has found a way to weave together the diverse threads of their life story into the work they now do.

Your Core Intention is about the energy and gift you bring to the world. A Core Intention is a precursor for your mission statement, where you get more specific about the "what" element.

This process of discovering your own Core Intention will unfold over time, as you go through the rest of the explorations and practices in this book. As Lauren wisely observes,

> It's so important to be patient with yourself. More clarity about my Core Intention only came to me after years of trying to figure this out. Then all of a sudden this piece from here and that from there came together and I realized, "Oh my god, that's what it's been all along, my entire life." That gives you a lot more freedom. Instead of cramming yourself into a box of "I'm a quilter," it opens all the boxes and you can do whatever helps you express that mission.

These next three explorations are intended to begin the process of helping you open to this level of inquiry.

CORE INTENTION EXPLORATION #1

FINDING CLUES

Choose a notebook that you'll enjoy writing in and take time to journal on the following questions. The paper can be lined or unlined. If you're a visual person, you may want to sketch or draw in your response to the questions. Another option is to have a friend ask you the questions, like an interview, then they can take notes on your answers or record you as you speak.

- What lights you up like a holiday tree?
- What makes your internal tuning fork vibrate at a high frequency?
- If your financial needs were taken care of and money was of no concern, what would you most enjoy doing with your day?
- What activities do you engage in that make you completely lose track of time?
- What comes so naturally and easily to you that you rarely think of it as a strength?
- If you knew you only had a year to live, how would you want to spend the majority of your time and energy? How about if you only had a month to live?

The more you're able to shift from analytical thinking to intuition, the more helpful this exercise will be in turning up clues about your Core Intention. You know that feeling when you're trying to take the lid off a jar that's very difficult to open? You might struggle with it in various ways, and then finally you find just the right angle with just the right strength, then the pressure inside the jar releases and that spot in the middle of the lid makes a satisfying "pop." That's what this is like.

You may find that some questions evoke more of an emotional and visceral response from you than others. That's great—spend most of your time on those questions. If you find it difficult to relate to a certain question, move on to the next one. Try coming back to it later to see if it lands differently with you, but don't worry if you can't relate to it.

Course graduate Jill Seidenstein shared how one of the questions impacted her:

> The question about the tuning fork really hit something that none of the other questions ever have. Here's how I responded:
> "Yesterday was a perfect example of what makes my internal tuning fork vibrate at a high frequency. I went to a writing workshop led by a fantastic and inspiring teacher. I was focused on improving my craft, which is what burns inside of me. Every time I go away and try to do something else, I keep returning to this. I want to write.

Being in a room with other writers, all learning and pushing our-
selves to improve put me on another plane of existence. I was wired
for hours after."

Keep these notes in a place where you can easily find them so that you
can refer to them in future exercises.

CORE INTENTION EXPLORATION #2:

WHAT ARE YOUR ACTION WORDS?

Look at the list of verbs below. As you look at each word, say it aloud
and allow at least ten seconds to sit quietly and notice how much or
how little you resonate with that particular word. Then write a number
next to it, using a rating scale of 1 to 5. If you feel nothing at all about
the word, give it a 1. If you're ready to jump out of your chair because it
resonates with you so strongly, give it a 5.

bridging	healing
brightening	inspiring
building	integrating
communicating	leading
connecting	listening
creating	learning
designing	loving
discovering	nurturing
embracing	organizing
empowering	playing
encouraging	protecting
facilitating	relating
giving	remembering
growing	restoring
guiding	teaching

Are there other verbs not included on this list that you want to add? Go for it!
   Now look at your numbers. Circle every word that you've rated with
a 4 or 5. Write these words down in your journal. You'll want to be able
to refer to them later when you craft your Personal Mission Statement.

If you have lots of words with a rank of 4 or 5, here's a way to narrow down your list to your top three words. Think about the absence of these activities in your life. If you were given the choice between going the rest of your life without being able to "discover" new things or without being able to "embrace" experiences, which would you miss the most? What can you absolutely not live without? Adjust your rankings accordingly and put an asterisk next to the words you would have the hardest time living without.

Now that you've identified three action words that carry a lot of charge for you, consider what each of those verbs is in relation to. For example, if "bridging" is high on your list, what do you feel called to bridge? Perhaps you feel strongly about bridging the gap between rich and poor, or bridging divisions between diverse faith traditions in your community, or something else. Write this down as well in your journal, for future reference.

Three of the strongest words on the list for me are "learning," "discovering," and "connecting." These words describe what makes me feel most alive as well as how I believe I'm here to serve others. I am at my best when I'm learning new things, and when I'm supporting other people to discover and connect. This has helped me to realize my Core Intention: to open hearts and minds.

CORE INTENTION EXPLORATION #3

A plethora of tests and surveys has been designed to help you get to know yourself better and to support career exploration. One tool that is especially relevant to discovering your Core Intention is the VIA Survey of Character Strengths. This free and simple self-assessment can help you to understand your core characteristics, the positive parts of your personality that impact how you think, feel, and behave.

The VIA Survey was created under the direction of Dr. Martin Seligman, the father of Positive Psychology, and Dr. Christopher Peterson, author of *A Primer in Positive Psychology*. The premise of the survey is that every individual possesses twenty-four character strengths in varying degrees. These strengths fall into six "virtue categories": Wisdom, Courage, Humanity, Justice, Temperance, and Transcendence.

You can access the VIA Survey online here: www.viacharacter.org. It should take you fifteen minutes or less to complete. After you've taken the survey, you'll receive a character profile; you can then consider how these strengths might inform your Core Intention.

For example, according to the VIA Survey, my top three character strengths are Creativity, Judgment, and Love of Learning. At first, I couldn't relate to Judgment—I take pride in being very nonjudgmental! But when I read the description it made sense: "Thinking things through and examining them from all sides are important aspects of who you are. You do not jump to conclusions, and you rely only on solid evidence to make your decisions. You are able to change your mind." And Creativity and Love of Learning reinforced what I was already guessing—that "discovery" and "learning" were essential ingredients of my Core Intention.

3. WHAT DO I NEED TO THRIVE?

A pivotal point in my own journey to a Liberation-Based Livelihood was taking a thorough inventory of my past work experiences—the good, the bad, and the ugly. Much like the fourth of the Twelve Steps for addiction recovery with its request to take a "fearless and searching moral inventory," this kind of inquiry can help us to see our patterns and also to notice the conditions we need to thrive in a workplace.

Clues about our Core Intention can be found here as well, as we become aware of the kinds of jobs or settings in which we felt the most alive, and when we felt drained.

You'll draw on the insights from this exercise throughout the remainder of the book, so make sure to allow yourself plenty of time to go through it with care and thoughtfulness, and keep it in a place for easy reference.

EXPLORATION: MINING FOR GOLD IN YOUR JOB HISTORY

1) List all the jobs you can remember (including volunteer positions).

2) Rank your level of "Excitement" and "Meaning" for each job.

Excitement: In general, how excited did you feel in that job? How eager were you to get out of bed and start each day of work?

Meaning: In general, how much did you feel a strong sense of meaning in this job that this job made the best use of your gifts/talents; and that you were making some kind of contribution?

Scale rating:

1=not at all 3=medium 5=incredible, off the charts!

3) For every job that you rank at 4 or above in both "Excitement" and

MINING FOR GOLD IN YOUR WORK HISTORY

1) List all the jobs you can remember (including volunteer positions).

2) Rank your level of "Excitement" and "Meaning" for each job.
   Scale ratings:
   1=not at all   3=medium   5=incredible, off the charts!

3) For every job that you rank at 4 or above in both "Excitement" and "Meaning," take a closer look and write reflections in the last column.

JOB	"EXCITEMENT" RANKING	"MEANING" RANKING	WHAT DO YOU NOTICE?

JOB	"EXCITEMENT" RANKING	"MEANING" RANKING	WHAT DO YOU NOTICE?

Other reflections and insights you get from doing this exercise:

"Meaning," take a closer look and write reflections in the last column. What exactly about that job helped you to feel that way? Was there a cause or issue that was being addressed and, if so, what was it? How did you contribute to that? What else do you notice? Other reflections and insights you get from doing this exercise.

Set aside at least one hour to do this exercise, and if you're able to give it more time, even better. Mining for Gold is a three-step process:

1. REMEMBERING

In the first column, list every job you remember having. Include volunteer positions such as serving on the board of a local organization and meaningful projects such as creating a piece of artwork or planting a community garden. Also think back on other significant responsibilities you've held that weren't necessarily attached to a paycheck—being a parent, taking care of your aging mom, cooking for a spiritual community. Sometimes our biggest clues about our Core Intention can be found in our extracurricular activities.

Don't worry if your list is very short, or on the long-ish side. This exploration will be valuable for you no matter how many or few jobs you can list.

2. RANKING

In the second column, rank each job/project for these two factors:

- Your level of excitement
- Your feeling of "being of use"

Use a 1–5 scale for ranking, with 1 being on the low end and 5 indicating a very high level of "excitement" about the job and a feeling of "being of use."

3. REFLECTING

Once you've ranked all of the jobs you listed. look for patterns and themes. Pay special attention to every job or activity that you ranked with a 4 or 5. What exactly was it about those jobs that was rewarding or frustrating? Can you see a common cause, issue, or problem that you were addressing? Use the third column to make note of your observations and discoveries.

If some of your jobs pop up with scores of "1" and "2," in which you were (or are) very unhappy, make some notes on exactly what it was that did not work for you—was it a toxic boss? An office with no windows? Low pay? Too much overtime?

Perhaps a certain job was a mixed experience—you loved some of what it included, but other parts of it were unpleasant. Note this as well. What factors could have been changed to make it a better fit for you?

Important note: This exercise may trigger some challenging emotions. As you review your job history, you may encounter internal resistance and doubts, thoughts such as these:

- Oh wow, what a bunch of terrible jobs I've had throughout my life. This is too painful to look at.
- I'm ___ years old and I still haven't had a job I've really loved. What's wrong with me?
- I'm a creative person and I don't want to put myself inside a box that defines me too narrowly.

Or … fill in the blank. Yep, I've been there, so I know just how weaselly our minds can be with this kind of inner work.

Remember the practice of "not spinning your story" from chapter 3? If your Mining for Gold review turns up a lot of jobs that weren't right for you, don't let yourself spiral into despair. It's okay to give yourself space to grieve and feel sad for a while, if that's helpful, but don't allow yourself to get stuck there. Here's another way to look at it: this information can help you get closer to understanding what conditions you need to thrive, and knowing what to say "no" to in the future.

This process is a lot like being a detective of your own life. You're looking for clues about what you need to fall in love with your work, as well as what you need to avoid.

Fall in Love with Your Work course participants over the years have dug up some valuable nuggets of insight through this exercise. Here are a few of them:

I was surprised by how high I ranked some of my early menial jobs, in terms of "being of use." Jobs like being a hostess at a restaurant or teaching English in Japan. I'm starting to see that I feel useful when I'm in a people-facing role. I hadn't noticed that before … I am curious what else I'll uncover!

A few words kept showing up for me about different jobs, projects, and volunteer placements: collaboration, support, connection, social, fun, creative. However, the one word that ties in with everything I have done is "service." This was such an obvious discovery for me but I just saw it in a whole new way.

I discovered that I thrive when there is clear intention and purpose (not just my personal one but with the project or organization), freedom to create, being around creative events, and being part of a team with equal time for independent work.

INTEGRATING KEY 1

Find a quiet place. Sit down with the following questions and see what answers arise. Use your journal to write down your observations.

- What is one belief or assumption you've carried about work that no longer serves you and that you want to release?
- After doing the explorations in this chapter, what's emerging as your Core Intention?
- What surprised you the most in your Mining for Gold review? What ingredients did you discover you need to thrive in your work?

A MEDITATION ON LOVE

A few months before the legendary jazz musician Louis Armstrong died, his doctor, observing that Louis was very ill and needed to conserve his energy, urged him to cancel a show he was scheduled to play in New York City. Louis resisted this instruction mightily. He told the physician, "My whole life, my whole soul, my whole spirit, is to blow that horn. The people are waiting for me, I got to do it, Doc, I got to do it."

Armstrong went ahead and played a two-week engagement at the Empire Room of the Waldorf Astoria hotel. He was hospitalized at the end of that time, and then died of a heart attack four months later. I like to think that he died as a happy man, knowing he was doing exactly what he was meant to do.

I'm going to lay a big spiritual lesson on you, one that I hope relieves a lot of pressure as you continue to clarify your Core Intention in this chapter and the rest of this book.

You are here on the Earth for one purpose only: to transmit Love. Yes, that's Love with a capital L, the kind that isn't limited to one person, that doesn't expect something in return, and that absolutely *must* be expressed. If it's not expressed, you'll feel it as a deep, nagging pain inside your soul. This is what Louis Armstrong was talking about, and his livelihood was a brilliant embodiment of that. This "Love with a capital L" is the biggest and most expansive way to understand Core Intention.

How you express this transmission of Love is uniquely yours—that's where your Core Intention comes in, as well as your Personal Mission Statement. You feel this when you experience it from someone else. I know someone who makes the most amazing apple pies. They are delicious, but the real secret ingredient is Love. Those pies are her way of transmitting Love and you feel it when you taste them.

Your work is the primary vehicle to transmit Love. You don't have to wait for the perfect job to do this. If your expression of Love is to listen deeply to people's stories, you can set your intention to do that as a janitor, if that happens to be your current job.

Take one more look at your "Mining for Gold" worksheet, this time through the lens of Love. In what kinds of jobs or projects did you feel that Love come shining through you?

CHAPTER 5   Key 2: Value Your Gifts and Time

Self-respect has nothing to do with the approval of others—who are, after all, deceived easily enough; has nothing to do with reputation, which, as Rhett Butler told Scarlett O'Hara, is something people with courage can do without... To have that sense of one's intrinsic worth which, for better or for worse, constitutes self-respect, is potentially to have everything .... Character—the willingness to accept responsibility for one's own life—is the source from which self-respect springs.

—Joan Didion

If you have a tendency to not ask for what you need in your workplace (and elsewhere), to tolerate unhealthy working conditions for too long, to offer your time and skills for less money than feels okay, this Key will support you in developing an internal compass that guides you to know when to say "yes" and when to say "no." This Key helps you to become a mindful steward of your time and energy.

The first time I read the above passage by Joan Didion, in my twenties, it stopped me in my tracks. The words hit much too close to home. It's an excerpt from an essay titled "Self-respect: Its Source, Its Power," published in *Vogue* magazine in 1961, which was coincidentally the year I was born. When I read this passage, I realized how much I would gauge my value in comparison with other people. This wasn't just my personal trip. I believe many of us grow up with this way of seeing "value," and most work environments are organized around it.

When I was a music therapist in a psychiatric hospital, there was a clearly defined pecking order among the staff. Psychiatrists were at the top, then psychologists, and then head nurses. After that came rehabilitation therapists like myself, and finally mental health workers. This hierarchy was related to salary as well as decision-making power. The psychiatrist on our treatment team made way more money than any of us. Even though he spent the least amount of time with the patients, he had the authority to make decisions that would impact everyone, staff and patients alike. Mental health workers spent the most time with the patients and knew them the best but received the lowest salaries. The reality was that each person had a vital role to play, but the system was set up to value some more than others.

During those years of working in the mental health system, I'd look at my colleagues with an MSW or a PhD and think, "If I just had that degree, I'd be happier in my work and I'd earn more money." I was seeking respect from titles, salary, and others' approval. In order to get those things, I exhausted myself by doing too much and trying to please everyone. I attended lots of professional trainings and conferences, but did so more out of panic that I wouldn't be "enough" unless I had more credentials than from a genuine love of what I was doing.

This is the paradigm of comparison and competition. Most of us live in it most of the time. It's hard not to in our society. This Key, Value Your Gifts and Time, invites you to step into another paradigm, one where you recognize your inherent self-worth and where you can make decisions about how you invest your time and energy based on that.

WHAT'S YOUR RELATIONSHIP TO THIS KEY?

Ask yourself the following questions to assess your current relationship with this key:

- How much is my sense of self-value based on external measurements, such as salary, job title, position in the company, number of Facebook friends, etc.?
- How often do I compare myself with others and base my value on these comparisons?
- Am I in a toxic job situation? How long have I stayed in this situation? Be as specific as possible; list the years, months, days if you can count 'em. What has kept me from moving on?

What does it actually mean to designate something as "valuable"? We are saying that it is worthy of our time and energy. We take care of the things we value, and we may go to great lengths to protect them against what might be harmful or destructive.

In a financial context, the more valuable we think something is, the more we are willing to pay for it. Value is subjective—what might be extremely valuable to me could be worthless to you.

Typically, we use measures like job titles, salaries, and popularity to determine our value. We think if we just work harder, we'll get promoted to a position that would pay us more and add to our prestige. If we spend more time on Facebook and say clever things, then we'll increase the number of our "friends" or "likes." We are forever trying to jump over a bar that gets raised higher and higher. These types of external measurements are subject to change and loss. Even though we may have the illusion of control, they are, for the most part, outside of our control. At any moment, any of those things upon which we've staked our value could shift or fall apart on us. When that happens, we may feel devastated.

What if you could rest in knowing that the source of your self-worth comes from inside of you, that it's not reliant on outside factors? How might your orientation to livelihood be transformed? How might your life be different? That's what this Key gives you a chance to find out.

Valuing yourself is intimately connected with self-respect, as Ms. Didion observes. As you become intimate with your Core Intention and develop a deeper regard for your own gifts and contributions, you will quite naturally become more protective of them in a positive way. You become more aware of how you spend your time, and you dedicate more of your resources toward that which you love.

As you engage in this process, your orientation toward your work can shift dramatically. Your capacity to value yourself has an impact on the standards you hold for the jobs you accept, as well as on your level of tolerance for jobs that are not a good fit for you or unfair working conditions. It also has an impact on your capacity to imagine what's possible. Your imagination is limited when you do not value yourself and your skills.

The more you value yourself, the more natural it becomes to set your compass toward work that expresses your Core Intention, and to say "no" to work that doesn't allow you a chance to offer your gifts, or that demeans you. You're more likely to "dismiss whatever insults your soul," in the eloquent words of Walt Whitman.

There's a beautiful paradox embedded in this Key. Knowing your own value from this internal perspective does not mean you value others less. One of the gifts of mindfulness practice is a deepening realization that we live in an interconnected world, that everything exists in relationship to everything else. That cereal in your morning breakfast bowl relies on the farmer who harvested the grains and the trucker who brought it to your grocery store. It also depends on the soil that nourished the plant, as well as the sun and rain that gave it what it needs to grow. It would be impossible to say that any one of those people or conditions is more important than another in making it possible for you to enjoy your bowl of cereal.

In the same way, as you begin to realize the inherent value of your Core Intention and the skills that accompany it, you understand that they don't make you "more" or "less" than someone else. This Key invites you to step into a paradigm that is based in mutual cooperation and appreciation, and invites you to take responsibility for your own well-being.

KEY 2 PRACTICES

1. RECOGNIZE YOUR WORTH

This recognition comes about through understanding your Core Intention and taking an inventory of what you have to offer—your innate gifts and skills. You began this process with Key 1, Become Intimate with Your Core Intention, and you'll continue it in this chapter (and beyond).

Look back once again at your Mining for Gold worksheet. This time, allow yourself to appreciate the breadth and depth of experiences you've had throughout your work life. No one else has traveled your path. Everything—joyful as well as difficult work experiences—has brought you to where you are today. Take a few moments to stop, breathe, and feel that truth.

Now take a look at the list of qualities below. As you reflect on your work history that you charted in Mining for Gold, notice the three qualities that you have brought into your diverse jobs, projects, and other undertakings. Which three have been themes that have shown up throughout your work history? If there is a quality you recognize in yourself that isn't on the list, add it.

Your Qualities

accepting	gratitude
adaptable	honest
adventurous	humor
analytical	integrity
appreciative	intuitive
assertive	kindness
being true to oneself	loving
bold	loyal
calm under pressure	mature

competitive	open-minded
conservative	patience
consistent	reliable
courageous	resourceful
creative	responsible
decisive	results-oriented
detail-oriented	risk-taker
enthusiastic	self-aware
ethical	self-confident
fair-minded	sensitive to others' needs
flexible	team-oriented
friendly	thorough
generous (with your time and energy)	visionary

Write these three qualities down in your journal. Then give yourself a dramatic reading. Stand in front of a mirror with your three words in front of you and notice what it feels like to say aloud, in a clear and confident way, "I am bold, creative, and honest." Or perhaps for you it's, "I am ethical, loyal, and sensitive to others' needs." Or whatever your three qualities are.

Allow yourself to appreciate how you have brought those qualities into the jobs and projects you've had throughout your life, and how other people have benefited from them.

Notice what language you use to think of yourself and describe yourself to others. Do you hem and haw about your skills? For example, do you say, "Well, I am a hairdresser but I'm just starting out." How does it feel different when you say, "I am a sought-after hairdresser." If one or two people received a great deal of value from their haircut with you, what you are saying is true. Even if you don't feel one hundred percent confident, this is a playful way to "fake it until you make it."

What's actually more important than your technical skill as a hairdresser (or administrative assistant, or web designer, or whatever you do) are these three invaluable qualities that you bring into it. There are likely a number of people who offer the same service or product that you do or something similar, but you bring something unique to the table. This is a chance to believe yourself into greatness.

As you internalize this appreciation of your gifts, you'll develop more confidence in communicating that to others and asking for what you need. Yael, who created Kulanu, the Zen Jewish Waldorf preschool, gives us a wonderful example of this:

I feel incredibly grateful to be able to support myself financially doing the work that I love. I know that the tuition fees I have set for Kulanu are on the high end of the going rate in our area, but I feel that what I am offering is unique and worth what I am asking. I bring not only my extensive training and many years of experience to this work but, also, my wholehearted self, my complete mindfulness, focused attention, and boundless love. That's worth a lot!

In establishing tuition fees, I try to find a balance between what parents can afford to pay and what I need to make this work of caring for their children financially sustainable for me. When I can, I offer parents partial barter arrangements. I have learned, though, that if I am going to forego some of my income, I need to make sure that I am receiving something of equally high value—that I really do need and want—in return.

2. ASK FOR WHAT YOU NEED

Now that you're getting a better sense of your true value, of what you bring to the table, it's time to get clear on what you need to support yourself in a way that honors your experience and the wisdom you hold.

Note that this support can take the form of financial compensation—such as salary or how much you charge for a service, product, or creation if you're self-employed—but it can take other forms as well.

Since financial support is fundamental for many of us, let's start with that.

PRACTICE #1: KNOW YOUR BOTTOM LINE

This is an actual number! Take time to add up everything that is a necessary monthly expense for you: housing, utilities, transportation, food, loans and/or mortgage payments, and any other financial obligations you have. This is your bottom line, the number you need to hold in mind any time you're in a situation where you're negotiating for your livelihood, such as talking with your boss about a raise, or to the person doing the hiring for a position you've been offered.

If you are a freelancer or self-employed, there are a few additional factors to consider in calculating your bottom line. Whether you are a private chef, an organizational consultant, an artist, or something else, there are expenses involved in making and offering your service or product. Some of these expenses are easy to forget—such as supplies necessary to carry out your trade or craft, professional training, contributions to your health insurance and retirement accounts, and travel expenses. Write these down and add them up so you have a better sense of what you actually need as you set a price for your service or product.

Another approach is to offer a sliding scale to clients and customers, which takes into account your financial needs as well as the needs of those with whom you work. It can be empowering to take charge of your business in this one-on-one way.

PRACTICE #2: ASK FOR THE AMOUNT THAT FEELS RIGHT TO YOU

This is an amount that takes into account your inherent value as well as the money you need to support yourself. Asking for this amount can be an edge for many of us who are used to underestimating our needs and worry that others may not be able to meet our expectations. If you have a longtime pattern of undervaluing yourself, here's a good rule of thumb: take the first number you come up with and then increase it by fifty percent. So if you're considering quoting a fee of twenty dollars an hour for work on a freelance project, up that to thirty dollars. If the annual salary you think you need is forty thousand, ask for sixty.

Potential customers and clients will usually request a proposal or bid from you. Again, make sure you know your bottom line (which you identified from the previous practice) as you set your fees and communicate this to them.

This may feel uncomfortable. That's good! Resist the temptation to jump out of that discomfort and instead take it as a sign that you're pushing your growing edges. Who knows, you might get what you're asking for!

Musician Jami Sieber talks about her experience of mastering the art of asking:

> When I do a show, I say, "My fee is two thousand dollars, and if you can't afford that, let me know." Earlier in my career, I would have said it was just six hundred. I now hold the lower fee as my bottom line. When people ask to use my music for a film, I'm not afraid to say, "It can be anywhere from a few hundred to a few thousand." It's about valuing my work, and recognizing I need to ask for what it is I feel I'm worth. I may not get it, but there are those times when they say yes, and it works! Don't sell yourself short.

It comes down to the value of the work, too. When I'm touring, I'm starting to recognize that the costs are greater than I think. I used to think if I got five hundred dollars for a gig, that was fine. Then I started to realize when I'm on the road I'm not taking into account that I have to pay for a car rental, as well as for my expenses at home, I need to put something in my IRA, and more. It's been hard to face that and realize I need to think about all these aspects.

PRACTICE #3: CONSIDER NONMONETARY FORMS OF SUPPORT

Compensation doesn't always have to come in the form of money. You might identify other factors that you need to support your capacity to offer your Core Intention to the world in a sustainable way:

- A clean and beautiful place in which to work.
- A flexible schedule that allows you to work from home one day a week so you can spend more time with your family.
- Enthusiastic support from your supervisor, coworkers, or others.
- Mentoring from someone whose work you admire and who can help you develop your skills.
- Referrals from happy clients and customers so that you will have more clients and customers!

What else comes up for you as you consider what you need? Review your Mining for Gold worksheet again. This time pay attention to the conditions that helped you to thrive in a workplace. You may be able to provide some of these for yourself, while others can be part of what you negotiate with those who want to support your work.

There may be strategic reasons why you give away something or offer it for less than you usually would. When I first created Fall in Love with Your Work as an online course, I spent a lot of time thinking about how to price it. Given the hundreds of hours I put into creating the course as well as the level of life experience and wisdom that I was drawing on, I set a ridiculously low registration fee. The first time I offered it, one of the course participants wrote to me, mentioned this low amount, and encouraged me to not undervalue myself. In fact, he paid more than what I was asking for the registration fee!

I had a good reason for setting the low fee, however, and it wasn't about undervaluing myself. I was trying something brand new (creating an online course), and it would have been easy for me to get hung up on that fact and not take any action to make it happen ("I've never done this before! Who would possibly want to pay for it?"). I wanted to make sure I went ahead and created the course without getting stopped by that hesitation. We'll look at this in more depth when we get to Key 3, Break Through Inertia and Take Action.

So for that first time around, I felt comfortable with the low fee because it allowed me to offer a "beta version" of the course and ask participants to give feedback about their experience. Their feedback was invaluable—it enabled me to improve the course for the next time around, and I got a chance to practice my teaching skills as well. The second time I offered the course, I raised the fee to one that was more reflective of its value and my growing expertise in teaching it.

3. CREATE YOUR ZONE OF CLARITY

The Zone of Clarity is a chart comprised of three sections: your unique value, your financial needs, and your other types of needs (e.g., referrals, office space, mentoring, etc.).

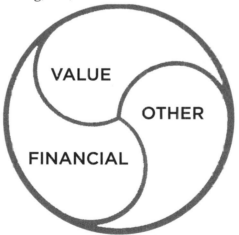

Review the first two practices in this chapter (Recognize Your Worth and Ask for What You Need) to find your content for these three sections. Go ahead and fill these in to create your personal Zone of Clarity chart.

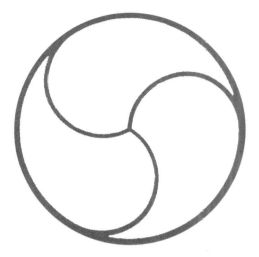

Your Zone of Clarity can serve as a visual tool that helps you know what to say "yes" and "no" to as work-related opportunities arise. You may want to print it out and hang it above your desk or in another location where you'll see it often. It's a great way to remind yourself what you have to offer, and what you need to receive to take care of your needs.

4. SAYING "NO"

The world is full of distractions that can pull you away from your Core Intention and out of your Zone of Clarity. Saying "no" is intended to bring in a protective energy so that you can keep your eye on the prize and give your full attention to work that matters. Fall in Love with Your Work graduate Martha Bouchier put it this way: "I need to say 'no' to situations and people who drain my energy, so I am able to give more to the people and situations who value what I offer."

You may find that people ask you to do things you're quite good at, or tasks that will primarily be in support of their work. While this isn't necessarily a bad thing, it's essential to check these requests against your Zone of Clarity and consider the consequences of saying "yes." By taking on a certain job or task, are you moving closer to or further away from your Zone of Clarity? As author Elizabeth Gilbert cautions, "No matter how alluring, no matter how beautiful, no matter how sparkling and fancy and delicious, do not say YES to other people's dreams."[8]

Fall in Love with Your Work graduate Karen Weber tells a wonderful story about this:

> *Even as a job I interviewed for clearly would become my life,*
> *meaning little time for what's essential to me, I caused myself suf-*

*fering trying to figure out how I could do it anyway. I told myself,
"I can make this work," while my body said NO and my dreams
said NO, and a dear friend said NO. I resolved not to do it and
the next day was told the job went to someone else. Whew!*

*Remember: just because you're good at something doesn't mean
you should do it.*

Here are some ways to work with this practice of saying "no."

PRACTICE #1: GIVE YOURSELF THE GIFT OF TIME

Refrain from automatically saying "yes" to whatever is offered to you
(such as a job) or asked of you (such as an invitation to help on a project).
Practice making this your default response:

*Thank you for asking. I need time to think about that before I can
give you an answer. Let me get back to you tomorrow (or next week
or whatever time frame feels right to you).*

This handy response allows you the gift of time so you can review your
Zone of Clarity and consider if this opportunity falls within it.

Martha shared that she makes it a practice to "take a breath or three
before saying yes to anything. I need to give myself a chance to really
think about it before I commit."

PRACTICE #2: SAY "NO" WHEN SOMETHING
FALLS OUTSIDE YOUR ZONE OF CLARITY

Once you've bought yourself some time, take out your Zone of Clarity
chart and look at it when you are faced with a decision about how to spend
your time and energy. Ask yourself if what is being asked or offered is
within your Zone of Clarity; if it's aligned with your Core Intention and
unique value; and if it meets your needs (both financial and nonmonetary).
Be ready to say "no" if it's not *and* be ready to stand behind your "no."

The first time I had a chance to practice saying "no" was when I was
negotiating for a salary during a job offer. I had never done this before.
Previously I would accept whatever was offered, just grateful that I had
been offered a position. This time I went in recognizing that I had a
unique combination of skills in qualitative research and contemplative
practice that were directly relevant to the position. I felt confident that

I could help the organization meet its goals, and I was able to "own" my value. I also had a clear idea of what I needed in terms of salary and benefits in order to support myself and to feel that my value was being recognized by the other party.

I communicated all this to the hiring person, including the salary I needed. The amount I requested was more than he was offering. I remained clear and firm about what I needed and was ready to let the opportunity go if the request wasn't met. At first, it seemed like the organization wasn't going to be able to come up with that salary. Then a few days later he called to tell me they were able to move some money around and they could meet my request. I'm convinced it was because I wasn't willing to settle for less than what I recognized my own value to be.

Sometimes the thing that falls outside our Zone of Clarity comes from our own ideas about what we "should" be doing. Lauren started out making quilts on commission for other people. She thought this was the perfect combination since she loved to quilt and she needed to make money. However, she soon discovered that the compromises involved in making a quilt to meet someone else's specifications stifled her creative expression. She reflected,

> *I kept feeling like I had to do them because I thought that should be my livelihood, but it was sucking my energy. Now I'm making what I want to make from an artistic perspective. I'd rather be working as an artist, and make what is related to what I'm trying to do and say with my life.*

Because Lauren had a background in tech work, she was able to pick up freelance projects in that industry to generate income, and found that kind of work didn't drain her creative juices the way the quilt commissions did. Even though the tech work wasn't her passion, it did provide her with the material resources to support herself so she could devote time to create quilts as an art form—a vehicle for her Core Intention.

5. INVEST IN YOURSELF

Investing in yourself is an important way to practice self-value. This investment often takes the form of money and/or time. You did this when you bought this book (or made the effort to borrow it from a friend or the library).

As you begin to recognize more of your potential, you may identify a number of things that will support this potential to evolve into a reality. Some of these might include:

- purchasing a piece of equipment you need for your work
- getting individual coaching for in-depth support
- taking professional trainings to sharpen your skills
- attending local networking events
- attending regional, national, or international conferences for more skill development, relationship building, and inspiration

Start a list in your journal to note these and other steps that will help you get where you want to be. What kind of investment will it take for that to happen, and what's getting in the way of making that investment? If your first answer is "I don't have the money" (a common one for many of us), what other creative ways can you manifest this step? For example, if you realize that you need a new computer to do graphic design work, could you set up a crowdfunding campaign and invite people who love your work to support you to raise funds for this? We'll explore more ideas like this in Key 5, Think Big and Make the Most of Your Resources.

The process of learning how to value yourself and your work is just that, a process. Don't expect to get it "right" from the start. Be patient with yourself and be willing to try things out and learn from the process. As you do this you may feel like you made a "mistake," as if you sold yourself short. Each time you put your work out into the world, you get another chance to discover what feels right to you and how to ask for that. Use every opportunity as a chance to see where old patterns of devaluing yourself may be coming up. Ask for help from others who have been down this path. Transformation is always possible!

INTEGRATING KEY 2

Find a quiet place. Sit down with the following questions and see what answers arise. Use your journal to write down your observations.

- What are the three qualities at the core of your value?
- What is your financial bottom line? How much money do you need each month to support yourself (and your family, if applicable)?

- What other nonmonetary forms of compensation would support you?
- What do you need to start saying "no" to?

A MEDITATION ON MONEY

This isn't a book about money, but it would be impossible to write about livelihood without touching on money as one important aspect of it, especially in relationship to how you value yourself. If you'd like to go into a deeper exploration of how you relate to money, I highly recommend *The Art of Money* by Bari Tessler, another book that takes this "inside-out" perspective.

Money is a powerful force in our lives. On the one hand it's only a piece of paper, a symbol. Yet it's such a potent one. We may relate to money as a material entity but nearly all of us bring so much baggage into the way we handle money that it's useful to explore it from a psychological and spiritual perspective.

Money is a gateway for both greed and generosity, for fear and love. Zen teacher Shunryu Suzuki Roshi once said, "In its wide sense, everything is a teaching for us: the color of the mountain, the sound of the river, or the sound of a motorcar. Each one is a teaching of Buddha." This is true of money as well; we can learn invaluable lessons about ourselves from how we handle money.

When we look deeply at money, we can see its subjective nature. Usually it's not the amount of it that makes us feel secure, but something else. (This is true up to a point; studies about happiness actually do show that a minimum amount of money to take care of basic needs is required for our emotional well-being. For example, in 2010 Princeton economist Angus Deaton and psychologist Daniel Kahneman published a popular study showing that $75,000 a year is the magic number for happiness; this number was updated five years later in 2015 to $83,000.)[9] There are billionaires who feel they don't have enough of it and there are people with a very modest amount who feel rich. As Coco Chanel once said, "There are people who have money and people who are rich."

Wealth is not limited to money. It might help to think of money as currency, in the sense that it's a means of mediating relationships and exchanges. Other forms of currency are time, energy, and love. All of nature is part of our wealth, in the biggest sense. What we do with these precious resources tells us a lot about who we are and what matters to us.

Money is typically equated with value. We may think that the higher a salary or hourly fee we are receiving, the more we are being valued. But this isn't necessarily true. Money isn't the only part of the value equation.

Even in professional fields that compensate employees well, the true cost of working in those jobs can be debilitating. If you consider your physical and emotional well-being as valuable, you'll realize you can't go along with that. Lauren, who formerly worked in the tech industry in the San Francisco Bay Area, said,

> I worked very long hours and made a lot of money. The longer I did that, the sicker I got. I had health problems that were mostly immune-related. I think that came from the stress of working sixty-hour weeks for fifteen years.

One common thread among those who have successfully created a Liberation-Based Livelihood is that they begin to understand that money does not have to be the main source of motivation for their work. When Lyndon first took Fall in Love with Your Work, he had this realization:

> Doing what I enjoy and am passionate about may not come with a big salary—I may even have to do it for free for a while, or for very little money. I started a meditation group and I loved doing that, but I didn't get paid a dime for it. But that built confidence that I could do something completely different, and it expanded my definition of what was possible. So even though I didn't make a living from my first efforts to do something different I'm still doing it four years later, and it's been a really good thing for our community.

Money *is* an important consideration, there's no denying that. But in order to open up the possibilities for a Liberation-Based Livelihood you need to find a way to reorient your perspective so that money is not the primary driver of your decisions.

One critical question to explore around your relationship with money is, how much is enough? Yael shared,

Having the resources and privileges that come from growing up in an upper-middle-class family enabled me to choose work throughout my adult life that felt meaningful to me in the service of others. I felt that the amount of money I earned was secondary to the value of the work I was doing. At this stage of my life, in my early sixties, while doing meaningful work is still my highest priority, earning enough money to support myself and my family has become a greater concern. Although I don't feel that I need a huge income, I do want to earn enough money to be able to cover my basic living expenses and, also, have enough financial resources to practice generosity for myself and others throughout my later years.

For Jami, a pivotal moment in her career came when she shifted her focus from trying to create music that would "make it," that would sell, and instead she began to trust that writing music inspired by her time with elephants in Thailand was what spoke most to her heart, whether or not it would ring up sales. Friends who were deeply inspired by what she was creating helped connect her to people who offered financial resources so she could make what became her breakthrough album, *Hidden Sky*.

Later in the book we'll look at the practical aspects of how to create a sustainable flow of income and ways to save on expenses so that you can take care of yourself and your family. For now, I invite you to simply try out the possibility that by understanding that money and value are not always synonymous, you'll give yourself greater leeway to discover innovative and surprising ways that your work can take form.

CHAPTER 6 — Key 3: Break Through Inertia and Take Action

No matter how wonderful our dreams, how noble our ideals, or how high our hopes, ultimately we need courage to make them a reality. Without action, it's as if they never existed.

—Daisaku Ikeda

The first two Keys give you the gift of slowing down and tuning into your inner wisdom so that you can discover what's truly important (your Core Intention), and then make choices from a place of insight rather than reactivity (through valuing your gifts and time). If you stay only in a place of reflection, though, you'll miss the other half of the dance. That's what this Key is about: Break Through Inertia and Take Action.

When I started my mental health career, it felt rewarding to offer my gifts to people in extreme states of emotional and cognitive distress, to learn new skills, and to work with a team of others who shared similar values. As time went on, though, the harsh reality of being part of a dysfunctional system wore away at me. I had a growing sense that a lot of myself had been left out of the equation. Parts of me that needed to be expressed, particularly my creativity, had nowhere to come out in my job. I was too exhausted at the end of the day to nurture that important piece of my life.

The realization that something had to change came long before I actually did something about it. This is perhaps the most painful time of this process—you know something needs to shift, but you aren't yet ready or able to take action that will lead to a shift.

In my case, it became clear that my work situation was detrimental to my physical, emotional, and spiritual well-being. While I could begin to see a pathway to a more fulfilling livelihood, there was still a long period of time when I couldn't bring myself to do anything about this.

In some instances, my resistance to action served a useful purpose and was instructive. At the time, pursuing a Master's in social work seemed like a logical next step. Yet, I couldn't even manage to complete an application for an MSW program. This was a big clue that it wasn't the direction I should take. My resistance—my procrastination and inability to apply for the next step in a mental health career—was a warning signal. Listening to my body and sensing its lack of excitement told me this wasn't the action to take.

I ran into another variety of resistance as I started to get clues about a new possibility for a career that I felt enthusiastic about—going to graduate school for anthropology at CIIS, the California Institute for Integral Studies. These kinds of questions arose:

- How can I let go of the steady income from my current job?
- How will I pay for graduate school?
- How can I let go of something I know how to do well to enter a field in which I'll be a complete beginner?

I kept tuning in to my excitement, even when it was tinged with anxiety. I realized that I could start taking small *action steps*, even if I didn't have definitive answers to all these questions. As a first step, I made a trip from my home in Oregon to San Francisco to visit the school and talk with the program director. Then I spoke with a graduate to hear about her experience. I walked myself through the resistance by telling myself that I was simply doing research. Nothing required a commitment, not yet anyway. Next I filled out the application. In contrast to my aborted attempt to apply for an MSW program, this process felt fun and exciting. I sent in the application and soon after a letter came in the mail to let me know I had been accepted. The time for a commitment had finally arrived, but by this time I felt ready and the answers to those questions were beginning to take shape. Each step on the way helped prepare me to get to a place where I could take the big step of saying "yes" and make a significant turn in my career trajectory. I have never, ever regretted this choice.

If you have a tendency to get great insights and ideas but those thoughts live only in your head, or if you get stuck in endless cycles of preparation without ever feeling like you're ready to move forward, this

Key will help you kick yourself into gear so you can take actions that will line up your livelihood with your Core Intention.

WHAT'S YOUR RELATIONSHIP WITH THIS KEY?

Ask yourself the following questions to assess your current relationship with this Key:

- When you get a great idea, how long does it take you to start putting it into action?
- Where in your professional life is there an action you could take that you've been delaying?
- What prevents you from taking this action?
- How often does this happen?

Imagine you've found a recipe for a sumptuous butternut squash soup. You can practically taste the rich flavors and the velvety texture, and you have a vision of sharing it with dear friends on a cool autumn night. A number of steps are involved in making this vision a reality: you need to go out and shop for the ingredients (perhaps you have some already in your pantry); cut the vegetables; sauté them; add herbs and spices; mix everything together in the right proportions; put the soup on the stove to cook; and finally invite friends over to share the feast. (You may also need to clean house!) But what if all you did was read the recipe, imagine this lovely scenario, and stopped there? That wouldn't be very satisfying at all.

As your Core Intention becomes clearer and you start to value your gifts, you'll discover that you actually need to *do something* to convert these insights into reality. This is the difference between imagining that delicious soup shared with friends and actually making it happen. That "something" you need to do might be asking your supervisor if you can switch to a flex-hours work schedule, or making a decision to leave your job and then following through with it, or starting your own business. Or another action.

We may be great at generating ideas, but when it comes time to actually make them happen, a million things seem to get in our way. Here are some of the forms this may take:

- Analysis paralysis: We spend so much time analyzing a situation that we delay taking productive action (or any action). We get bogged down in tweaking the same details over and over,

or we endlessly review the data in front of us without doing something about it.
- Perfectionism: We want to get everything "just right" before we send out our résumé, or launch our website, or share our project with a prospective partner or funder, or …
- Fear of failure: We keep ourselves safe by not ever moving toward our goal, because that way we don't have to risk failing at it. Fear of success is a close cousin. How might our lives change if this actually *does* succeed?

As you read through these avoidance modes, did you feel any wave of recognition move through you about any one of them? Or perhaps you might experience a combination of them. Are there other ways that you trip yourself up on the way to taking action?

By becoming aware of the kind of self-talk you engage in, you may realize that excuses you make for not taking action aren't always based in reality. The adage "Don't believe everything you think" rings true here. Sharyn, a writer and musician, based in the San Francisco Bay Area, shared her story:

> Sometimes I think, "I can't solve this problem." It's more effective to think, "I haven't solved it yet." For example, I am well qualified to teach Natalie Goldberg's writing practice and have her blessing, yet I have had trouble attracting students and finding a venue where I can teach. I tell myself things like, "Nobody knows me" and "I haven't published anything" and "The Bay Area is a tough, competitive environment for teachers."
>
> None of this is precisely true. I belong to an extended writing and meditation community and a large folk music community, and I have three hundred and some friends on Facebook. So some people know me. I have published songs and letters to the editor and poetry, so it is not strictly true that I have not published anything. The Bay Area may be this or that kind of environment, but I don't really know that. I haven't solved these problems yet; that doesn't mean I can't solve them.

The first step is often the most difficult. Once we begin to move in any direction, a momentum begins to take hold, like a tractor beam that pulls us along to the next step and the one after that, without our needing to know all the details. When we anchor ourselves in our Core

Intention and commit to acting in a way that will bring it out into the world, amazing things can happen. Jami Sieber related this story:

> *In 1994 I made my first solo album,* Lush Mechanique. *The steps I took to make this happen were huge for me. I took on a ten thousand dollar loan from a friend. Immediately after its release, Ferron invited me to tour with her as a backup musician and it was on that tour that the CD really entered the world with lots of sales. What became clear to me as I look back over the years was that with every step I made, doors opened that I couldn't have predicted. In some ways I didn't even plan my steps, I only knew that I had to do something. I had the intention to do music, to make the CD, and then doors opened.*

The sport of rock climbing is a wonderful metaphor for how this energy of taking action unfolds. When rock climbers make their way up the side of a mountain, they start by locating a foothold that will give them some stability and a way to find the next foothold. They can see the mountaintop, and they realize there are multiple paths that lead to that destination. One axiom of rock climbing is that if you want to move forward, you have to let go of where you are. You need to take that next step, even if you're not exactly sure how you will get to the top. Every step reveals more information about what needs to happen next—but you won't get that information unless you make a move. Even if you have to backtrack to a foothold you used before and take an alternate route, you are still making progress.

Lyndon Marcotte, whose action step was to start a meditation group in his community, said,

> *There's a certain element of faith in it. You need to trust that there's something out there for you even if you don't know what it is, or what direction to go in. There are risks and costs to be paid, whether it's a smaller salary or giving up security or certainty— as if we have any of that anyway. You're sacrificing a professional identity to explore new options and make yourself over again.*
>
> *I found that I had to be willing to be satisfied with small changes, to make mistakes and not be completely undone by it. You're just trying to figure it out as you go along. It's important to have patience and compassion for yourself. These are tools and skills that you learn through a meditation practice. I don't know how anyone could make changes like this without it!*

As you work with this Key, it's quite likely that you'll become more intimate with the sources of your fear. We'll explore these in more depth in Key 4, Make Friends with Uncertainty.

KEY 3 PRACTICES
1. NAME WHAT'S GETTING IN YOUR WAY

Knowledge is power—we can't change what we don't recognize.

Your avoidance strategies can actually help you to understand what's getting in your way. In Thich Nhat Hanh's practice communities, we often ring a "mindfulness bell" to remind us to return to our breath. The moment you notice one of your avoidance strategies in action, you can use it as a kind of mindfulness bell to prompt you to acknowledge that there's something that needs closer attention. It may be that you are simply fatigued, and your procrastination is telling you it's time to take a break and come back to this step later when you are refreshed. Or it may be telling you that you're hitting resistance or fear that is blocking you from taking action. Or maybe it is something else.

What do you notice you do to put things off? What activities do you engage in? Make a list of the three biggest culprits. For example, if I catch myself spending endless time on Facebook or getting lost on Internet bunny trails, I can be pretty sure that I'm finding ways to delay taking action. That's my signal to stop and ask myself, "What's really going on here?"

Once you catch yourself avoiding action through one or more of the activities on your list, your body and physical cues can be a doorway to learn more about what's happening.

Here's a simple practice that can shed more light on your inner process:

a) When you find yourself engaging in one of your avoidance activities, gently stop what you're doing. Please don't judge yourself as "bad." Instead, take this as an opportunity to learn.

b) Close your eyes and take three deep breaths. With each breath, see if you can send oxygen to every cell of your body.

c) Notice what's going on in your body. Are there any spots that feel particularly tense? Again, just notice, without judgment.

d) Ask yourself: What's true for me right now? And then wait a moment or two to see what emerges. The response may come in the form of words, or it may be a sensation in your body, or something else. Stay open.

e) You may want to write down your reflections on this practice in your journal.

Sam Watts, a Fall in Love with Your Work graduate, describes a variation on this practice that he uses:

> *If I can remember to check in with my body, I often feel a heaviness in my chest when I'm delaying or ignoring something important. I like to do a practice of a "mind sweep" when I feel particularly bogged down. This involves writing down the things that feel heavy and then addressing as many of those as I can, either through an action or some kind of acknowledgment. This has helped me to free up space and to notice when there are blocks that are causing more angst than growth.*

At the same time, I encourage you to not get *too* hung up in trying to figure out *why* you can't take action. Some insight is definitely useful, but even reflection can turn into a handy vehicle for putting off something that you know you need to do.

2. TAKE BABY STEPS

A goal or project might seem so huge that we don't know where to even begin. When this is the case, it helps to use the following three basic project-planning principles to make things more manageable:

1. "Reverse Engineering"

Start with your end point, then think backward. What is the next-to-last thing that needs to happen to get there? And then what needs to happen to get to the point before that? And so on.

For example, let's say your Core Intention is to nourish people and you also love to cook. When you go through the Personal Mission Statement process in chapter 10, you envision a home-based catering business that features delicious organic foods. Your end goal is to open up this business and reach potential customers. Using "backward engineering," here are some steps you'll need to take:

- create marketing materials such as brochures and a website
- contact your city's health department for an inspection of your home kitchen and get the necessary permits

- research the kind of equipment you'll need in your kitchen
- take a course at your local community college in safe food preparation

There are likely other steps as well. This strategy breaks a big idea down into smaller components and gives you an idea of the sequence that you're setting up for yourself.

2. Make Your First Step as Small, Simple, and Unthreatening as Possible

When I begin to envision a new project, my very first step is to make a folder on my computer with the title of that project. Making this kind of physical container for my vision helps to ground it, even if I am not sure what needs to happen next. It may seem like such a small step, but it's an important one!

Note that small does not equal insignificant. In her book *Micro Habits for Major Happiness,* Indigo Ocean Dutton describes how powerful these tiny behaviors can be in helping you to overcome inertia. In order to fulfill our intentions and meet our goals, we usually need to develop new habits (and quit some old ones). Micro Habits do just that. As Dutton points out, if you set up a Micro Habit that takes an average of no more than five minutes a day, your chances of sticking to it over time are quite good. For example, if your goal is to have a healthy savings account, a Micro Habit might be to transfer five dollars from your checking to your savings account each Friday.

It's also essential to feel an emotional connection with your intention or goal. Having a healthy savings account, on its own, may not be the primary motivator for you. The "why" underneath that goal is that it's very important for you to have a stable financial base so you can take care of your family. That motivation will fuel you to continue your Micro Habit day after day, week after week, and that consistency will create momentum. This "why" is also what your Core Intention provides, as you take small but important steps to move toward your Liberation-Based Livelihood.

3. Write Down This List of Steps

The act of writing this list is essential. When you put something in writing, it signals to your brain that you are committed to an intention or goal; it's a contract you make with yourself.

This list will evolve over time as you learn more about what's required for your particular action, and also work with the realities of your resources. Like the rock climber, you may find that a foothold presents itself to you on a different path than what you originally planned. That's okay. This is about moving closer to your end point in the way that most makes sense given the conditions that are present in each moment. As Dr. Martin Luther King, Jr., said, "Faith is taking the first step even when you don't see the whole staircase."

3. CREATE THE ENVIRONMENT THAT SUPPORTS YOU TO TAKE ACTION

We all have conditions that bring the best out in us and conditions that bring out the worst in us. If you're prone to procrastination because your office space is a mess and you "just can't think," your first step is to clear out that clutter. If energetic music helps you be in a mental space where you are more likely to get things done, put it on. If you work best when you're by yourself, make sure to block out alone time on a regular basis—once a day, once a week, or whatever frequency is realistic for you. If you do better when people are around you, head to a coffee shop. Become familiar with the ingredients that work best for you and put them in place.

Fall in Love with Your Work graduate Karen Weber decided one of her first action steps was to order a work desk that would fit in her small house. "I'm someone who loves having a dedicated space to work on with room to spread out. Currently I'm working on my small kitchen table and I am so excited to be getting this new desk and setting up a work space on it."

4. REMOVE THE ELEMENT OF CHOICE

Decision fatigue can be another obstacle to taking action. We are faced with so many choices about how to spend our time that we can freeze up and do nothing. Lauren noted how important this was for her:

> I need to minimize the number of decisions so that it becomes instinctive and I don't have to think about it. I need to remove mundane daily decisions as much as possible so I can use my brain for the important stuff, for the work that matters to me. Decision fatigue is real!

You can create routines that minimize some of those choices. For example, if the action you want to take is incorporating a consistent meditation practice into your life, write out a schedule of what you will do each morning and where meditation falls in that time frame. It might look like the following practice:

WRITE A SCHEDULE

7:00 a.m. Wake up
7:15 Take a shower
7:30 Put water on for tea
7:35 Meditate for ten minutes
7:45 Enjoy tea and make breakfast
8:15 Leave for work

Post the schedule in your bedroom so it's the first thing you see each morning. Invite yourself to simply follow the schedule, without having to make any decisions.

You can take a similar approach to other actions such as allocating more time to make your art, practicing a skill like active listening, or reaching out to a potential employer.

5. GIVE YOURSELF A DEADLINE

I have a love/hate relationship with deadlines—perhaps you do too. The word itself feels so morbid! Deadlines can be annoying when they feel like they inhibit our freedom. But there is a gift hidden within them—they can prompt us to get moving and remind us that procrastination is actually a bigger barrier to our freedom. When held in the right spirit these kinds of time lines can be life giving, not death inducing. Come up with your own language: lifeline, guideline, target date. What other phrases can you use that feel more positive to you?

Practice with setting mini deadlines, which is like running sprints. If you've got a to-do list, give yourself a set amount of time to complete the first item on it, like this: "In the next ten minutes, I will call my dentist." See how good it feels to actually meet those mini deadlines and cross tasks off your list.

In a similar way, find something that will give you just the kick in the pants you need to get yourself going. This book owes its existence to a kick-in-the-pants practice! It started when I was taking a class about instructional design and how to be a more effective teacher. The instructor offered us a powerful incentive: if we came up with an idea for our own course before the end of the six-week class, she would promote it on her website. I really wanted to take advantage of this chance to get my work out to thousands of people, so I cooked up the idea for an online course called Fall in Love with Your Work.

Once I'd created a course description and it was advertised through the teacher's website, much to my surprise and delight people started to sign up. This meant that I had to create the course and figure out a platform to deliver it.

In its first incarnation, Fall in Love with Your Work was a thirty-day course and thirty people registered for the inaugural run. When we started, I had only written the first seven days of the daily email lessons. I was literally creating the course on the fly, writing as fast as I could to stay ahead of the participants. The beautiful thing about this process was that I felt completely alive in my creative juices. I crafted each email lesson in response to the questions and challenges that participants were sharing with me, staying a few steps ahead of them. To this day, I believe that's what gave this framework vitality and relevance to those seeking to shake up their professional lives. Taking action became a joyful process of creation.

INTEGRATING KEY 3

Find a quiet place. Sit down with the following questions and see what answers arise. Use your journal to write down your observations.

- What is your go-to avoidance strategy? Which one of the practices in this chapter would you like to try first to break through that pattern?
- What small step can you take today to move you toward your vision of a Liberation-Based Livelihood?

A MEDITATION ON TIME

Our relationship to action has a lot to do with our relationship to time. Perhaps, like me, you tend to fall on the side of putting things off and you may be in some denial about time, thinking that it's endlessly available. If you don't get to something today, you'll do it tomorrow. Or next week. Or next month. Or, more likely, never. On the other hand, if you fall on the side of impulsivity, you may feel scarcity around time, that there will never be enough of it, so therefore it's better to do something—anything!—right now, without carefully considering the impact of your action on yourself and others.

There is some validity to both orientations. When we step out of a linear view of time, there is a beautiful paradox: You have all the time in the world … and your life could end tomorrow. Both statements are true.

Mindfulness practice teaches us how to live from a place that honors both those truths. The more you sit on your meditation cushion, spend time on your yoga mat, or whatever your practice is, you learn how to not be rushed and yet to know that there comes a time when it's important to act. You experience the timelessness of each moment; at the same time you touch into impermanence. You begin to understand what Harvard professor and author John Kotter calls "healthy urgency," a force that motivates individuals and groups to act in a sustained and powerful way.[10] You develop a more finely tuned connection to your body and mind, which helps you to discern between the kind of resistance that is a protective warning signal and the kind that is getting in your way.

I am reminded of the chant we recite at the end of each night of Zen practice during a long retreat:

> *Life and death are of supreme importance—*
> *Time passes swiftly and opportunity is lost—*
> *Let us awaken—awaken.*
> *Do not squander your life.*

Life is precious, and it is measured out in moments. Can you be aware of what is happening just now, just where you are sitting, without adding any other layers or stories to it? What is most important to you in this moment?

CHAPTER 7   Key 4: Make Friends with Uncertainty

When I dare to be powerful, to use my strength in the service of my vision, then it becomes less and less important whether I am afraid.

—Audre Lorde

The possibility of moving in any new direction related to livelihood can be thrilling. At the same time it can evoke anxiety, nervousness, unsettledness, and even absolute fear. The emotional charge that comes when we face uncertainty is one of the most common reasons we get stuck on Key 3, Break Through Inertia and Take Action, and end up settling for the status quo. That's why this task of befriending the unknown gets a chapter all its own.

In 2003, I went through a turbulent career transition. Unlike my earlier shift out of the mental health field, this one was not of my own choosing. It came during a period of time when everything else in my life fell apart.

My seemingly solid relationship with my partner at the time ended in a painful way. Because I was living in her house, I lost my home too. *Thank goodness*, I thought, *at least my job is the one stable point of my life.* I had worked at this small nonprofit in the San Francisco Bay Area for a number of years, first as an associate editor of their journal, then as executive director of the organization, and then as senior editor. That fall, along with a number of other staff, I received notice that we were being laid off. I was devastated. In combination with the breakup, it made my year truly awful, like the year that Queen Elizabeth II famously described as an *annus horribilis*, when three of her children went through very public marital discord and, to top it off, Windsor Castle caught fire.

As I stepped into the unknown territory of unemployment, I considered my next steps. I applied for a number of positions, but all this was unfolding just as the economy was in a major nosedive. The response to my great résumé? Crickets.

I still remember sitting up in bed late one night in my San Francisco apartment, a stream of excited energy pulsing through me, when I realized I didn't have to wait for someone else to hire me. I could create my own "job"—I could start a business based on the skills I had developed and draw on the network of people I had cultivated in previous years. In a flash it came to me: the name of the business would be Five Directions Consulting, a reference to the direction that many cultures designate in addition to the four cardinal directions (north, south, east, and west). This fifth direction represents the center, or "here." I intended the name to convey the reflective element that is at the heart of all my work.

I imagine Moses felt something similar when the Ten Commandments were delivered to him on stone tablets. I felt incredibly humbled and hugely important, all at the same time. I stayed up until the wee hours of the morning putting together a rudimentary website for this brand new business—which didn't have any clients. I had no idea what would or should happen next, but I was riding a wave of excitement as I took the first steps to launch my business.

In the years since that moment of inception, I've had to learn how to surf many more waves of uncertainty. I left the container of all that was familiar to me in a work environment: the structure of going into an office from nine to five every day, of having a relatively clear set of expectations about what I was expected to accomplish, and of receiving a regular paycheck.

All that was traded in for the roller coaster life that is the reality for many small business owners. Every work day, I am the one who needs to figure out what my priorities will be, how and when the next round of income will come in, what I'll be creating next to offer my clients, and how I will find those clients. Some months the work and income flows in with ease; other months can be a struggle.

This way of working requires a level of attentiveness, innovation, and courage that I rarely had to muster when I worked for someone else. It's not easy, but I've felt more present and alive and a feeling of true joy as I create my own work from day to day. When I began on this path in 2008, I could never have foreseen the places I'd go and the people I'd have the honor to serve as clients. I would never have imagined that I would create two online programs, Fall in Love with Your Work and

Waking Up to Your Life. All of this transpired because I kept leaning into uncertainty and staying open to possibilities.

If you find yourself freezing up with fear at the thought of making a change in your work, this Key can help you see uncertainty as a place ripe with creativity and potential. That doesn't mean you'll never feel apprehension about making big changes. But with practice, you can turn uncertainty into your ally rather than an enemy.

Everyone has their own relationship with certainty, and I don't want to assume what's true for you. It may be that you have a very high need for consistency and predictability, and that's fine. However, if you're that kind of person and you have no interest in renegotiating your relationship with uncertainty, the rest of this book will probably not work so well for you. However, if you're curious about how you can turn uncertainty from an enemy into a friend, let's keep going.

WHAT'S YOUR RELATIONSHIP WITH THIS KEY?

Ask yourself the following questions to assess your current relationship with this key:

- Imagine you're traveling to a foreign country that you've never visited before. You get off the plane, go through airport and border protocols, and then you're out on the streets of this new place. What is your default setting? Do you move into the experience with curiosity and exuberance, happy for the opportunity to try something new? Do you hang back, waiting to get a sense of what this place is about before you do anything? How else do you respond? Or is this a trip you could never imagine taking?
- When you consider making a major change in your livelihood, such as quitting your job and seeking a new one, what emotions come up for you? What is the intensity of these emotions? Do they feel relatively easy to navigate, or are they overwhelming?
- How open are you to seeing uncertainty in a new light?

One of the biggest obstacles to creating or finding work that we love is not being able to tolerate much uncertainty. We feel like we need a guarantee of where our next paycheck will come from, what will be expected of us on the job, what kinds of responses we can rely on getting from our supervisors and coworkers. We aren't willing to sit in a space of not knowing. We want it all tied up in certainty.

Except that we really don't. We yearn for the feeling of satisfaction and self-sufficiency that comes from facing challenges and meeting them. We long to get in touch with our own untapped source of strength and creativity.

To be a writer, a good one, you have to learn how to lean into uncertainty. Every time you open your journal to a blank sheet of paper, you have no idea what will come out. Rather than relying on rote formulas or what worked before, you need to venture into unfamiliar territories with an open and curious mind if you want your work to be animated with vital energy.

To have a Liberation-Based Livelihood you need to do the same thing. I'm guessing that one of the reasons you picked up this book is because you're drawn to the possibility of dramatically changing your work life—as well as a bit terrified by that same possibility. Change can be scary, especially when it comes to our livelihood, because it's so connected to our identity and our sense of financial security. You don't know what might happen, and so many things could go wrong:

- You could approach your boss with ideas for improving your work situation and the conversation could go terribly and make things worse.
- You could leave your job and be caught high and dry with no income.
- You could start your own business only to have it fail miserably.

We have a primal need for security, and it's important to recognize that. It's helpful to realize there are ways to mitigate risk. For example, if you discern that leaving your job and starting your own business is what you really, *really* want to do, you can set it up as a "Side Hustle" first—slowly dipping your foot into self-employment waters while continuing to work at your day job. You can become more intentional about putting things in place (like a healthy savings account) that will enable you to make the leap when the time is right. This doesn't have to be an all-or-nothing proposition. If you're going to jump out of a plane, it makes sense to prepare your parachute! We'll explore these strategies more in chapter 11, Navigate the Three Pathways to Liberation-Based Livelihood.

But there's a deeper spiritual layer here that's worth exploring. Uncertainty can stop us in our tracks. Yet those places where we have no idea what will happen next are the places wide open with potential. When we think we know the answers, there's not much room for anything to come in, and that includes inspiration and surprise. The gifts come when we can hang out in that space of not knowing.

Jami Sieber reflected on her process of preparing to travel to Thailand, after she accepted an invitation to play cello with the elephants of the Thai Elephant Conservation Center:

> *I don't know what led me to ask this question, but I wrote to Richard, the person who invited me to come to Thailand, and asked, "How do I prepare to play music with the elephants?" All he said was, "Go to your elephant self." Now I realize that was the greatest thing I could have ever done, to recognize I don't really know how to do this. So what question can I ask that will lead me to be open?*
>
> *I could have showed up in Thailand thinking, "All I need to do is play music and then the elephants will come." And I wouldn't have learned a thing. But I went there with this guidance to "go to my elephant self." I went in with questions, with unanswered wonder.*

The first of the three tenets of the Zen Peacemaker Order is "Not-Knowing." Bernie Glassman, cofounder of the ZPO, describes it like this, "Not-Knowing is entering a situation without being attached to any opinion, idea, or concept. This means total openness to the situation, deep listening to the situation."[11]

The other two tenets are "Bearing Witness" and "Taking Loving Action." These tenets were developed to transform social service into spiritual practice, but they can also inform how we approach our livelihood. Glassman explains more about what he means by "Not-Knowing":

> *Not-Knowing has nothing to do with knowledge. My sense is that one should have as much knowledge as possible. Learn as many languages as you can. Study as many fields as you can. Penetrate as deeply as you can. Learn all the tools and the techniques ... . Not-Knowing is simply not being attached to any particular piece of knowledge. In the same way, it is also not rejecting any piece of knowledge. You hear something and say "Ah! That's ridiculous! Forget it!" If you hear something, try responding, "Well, maybe that is possible also." "Oh! That's another way of looking at it."[12]*

This openhearted and playful take on relating to uncertainty is a wonderful entryway into practicing with this Key.

KEY 4 PRACTICES
1. LEARN HOW TO SURF

It's helpful to think of anxiety and fear as physiological energies that flow through us rather than solid and unchanging states of mind or emotions that get a grip on us. Our nervous system is wired for protection, so it's perfectly natural when a fight-or-flight response gets activated in the face of unknown or potentially risky scenarios. As humans we are also gifted with the cognitive capacity to reframe that warning signal. We can think of it as a wave of energy we can surf to help us take action, rather than something that makes it impossible for us to do anything. Essentially what we are doing is converting anxiety into creative energy. As Jon Kabat-Zinn, creator of mindfulness-based stress reduction (MBSR), once said, "You can't stop the waves, but you can learn to surf."

The very best way to learn how to surf is your contemplative practice. The mindfulness you cultivate through practice helps you slow down your mental and physical processes so that you don't revert to habitual reaction, but rather you can try out new responses.

Here's the basic surfing practice:

- Stop and reconnect with your body and breath.
- Notice what emotions and thoughts arise as you consider this situation of uncertainty, this new possibility.
- If fear and anxiety dominate your emotional landscape, ask yourself:
  » What is the worst possible thing that could happen? How could I respond to that if it does?
  » Have I dealt with situations like that before? What internal resources did I draw on to handle those situations?
  » What other resources are available to me as I enter into this situation?
  » Once again, return to your body and your breath, and reconnect with your natural strength and stability.

Fall in Love with Your Work graduate Martha Bouchier's story is a wonderful example of how to convert anxiety into creative energy:

*After a fifteen-year hiatus, I was invited to perform onstage
again with my band. I was panicking about it months before and
worked myself up into such a tizzy that I could barely function.
A few days before the performance there was this moment when I
just let go of my fear. I was worn out. I said to myself, "Whatever
happens, it will be fine."*

*The day of the performance came and I was the least nervous
of my bandmates—I was just excited. I got up on stage, the music
started, and I realized that so many of my friends and family
were there supporting me. I wasn't alone, I had these great people
with me on stage, we had practiced, and we were prepared. It felt
wonderful being up there after so long, like something I had been
missing and didn't know until that very moment. It was amazing and a real turning point for me.*

*I still struggle with fear, anxiety, and self-doubt but I never
experience any of those feelings when performing. I'm always just
excited. So now in any situation where I'm nervous I try to turn
it into excitement. There is a fine line between the two, and it's
easy to cross if I inject joy into it.*

2. PUT THE DRAGONS IN A CORRAL

Okay, let's tread a bit more into the thoughts and emotions that come up
as you consider making a big change in your professional life. Think of
these as the dragons of doubt and fear that inevitably show up when you
are engaging in a transformative process. While you want to tame these
dragons rather than feed them, it *is* important to recognize them, look
them in the eye, and then bless and release them. Denial is not helpful.

Here are a number of "dragons" that might come to visit as you start
to enter the land of uncertainty:

- I need the security that my current job offers me.
- I'm afraid if I start something new, it will be a failure.
- I'm afraid if I ask my boss for better working conditions or a raise
  in my salary, they will refuse and things will be even worse.
- I'll never find another job where I make as much money as I
  do now.
- I don't know if I have the energy to start my own business and
  keep it going.
- I don't know what I have to offer that anyone would want to buy.

What do you feel are your biggest obstacles? Bring out your journal and make a list of the concerns that come up for you as you consider changes you want to make.

Now here's the practice: Find a way to contain those obstacles in your writing—literally. This is the corral for the dragons. If you are handwriting in your journal, draw a box around the perimeter of your journal page and keep this list of dragons inside that area. You can do the digital equivalent if you're on a computer by creating a frame around the page. The purpose of this box? To remind you that these obstacles don't need to rule your life. They may be genuine concerns that need to be addressed, but they are all *workable*. That's the key word.

3. BEST-CASE SCENARIO

"Monkey mind" is a phrase often used in Buddhism to describe our mind when it's in an undisciplined state. We can talk ourselves into some scary places when we let our monkey mind run rampant and spin out the worst-case scenarios.

If you're going to put all that energy into imagining what could happen, why not move in the other direction? You can turn around that tendency to spin a story and instead come up with the "Best-Case Scenario." What is the *best* possible outcome of stepping into this situation? What if it succeeded beyond your wildest dreams? What might that look like, and what does it feel like? Be as specific as you can, but also let your imagination run wild!

Play with this for a while. It may feel a bit uncomfortable if you're not used to thinking this way, but it's great calisthenics for your spirit. You're stretching yourself into a new, courageous way of being in the world.

4. GIVE YOURSELF A BREAK

If you've gotten this far in this book as well as in your own process, you're now doing the "heavy lifting" of facing and transforming some very old beliefs and habits. That's amazing—congratulations! It's important to acknowledge that this can be difficult work. Don't expect yourself to hang out in that cauldron of intensity day in and day out without a break. Good doses of self-care and levity are essential to add into the mix.

Karen Weber, another course graduate, shared her story:

> Recently I moved from the Hudson Valley in upstate New York after nearly twenty years. I left my job, community, friends, former teacher, way of life, and living space, and came to Santa Fe with a vision of what I needed, and a couple of contacts. There has been a lot

of uncertainty in making this move. The uncertainty began inter-
nally as I questioned all that was around me, all that I was involved
with, all that I needed, and then it spread externally toward my basic
survival needs. At times it has been very lonely and also painful, like
a long dissolution of the past to give way to the future. I tried to have
both, holding to the past and what I knew to be changing within me
leading to the future, and it just meant being stuck.

In this situation, I found taking small steps each day to be essen-
tial, being present to what could happen that day. Keeping the energy
moving in small ways, balanced with periods of "time off" is import-
ant for me because I can worry, overthink, and become paralyzed.

What's on your self-care list? What activities help you to replenish your
energy and shift your perspective? Here are some possibilities:

exercise • dance • prayer • meditation • listening to music
time with a friend • being in nature • cooking healthy food • travel

Start your own self-care list in your journal. Turn to it whenever you begin
to feel yourself getting dragged down into despair or other dark places.

And don't underestimate the power of a sense of humor—laughter is
a wonderful release valve for anxiety. Another course participant remembered a friend who taught her an important lesson: It's okay to feel a little
scared and anxious about the unknown. When that friend made phone
calls to new people, she'd give herself a pep talk: "Be brave, little chicken!"
Remember to laugh at yourself, in the kindest and most gentle way.

INTEGRATING KEY 4

Find a quiet place. Sit down with the following questions and see what
answers arise. Use your journal to write down your observations.

- As you get clearer on a vision for your Liberation-Based
  Livelihood, what edges of uncertainty show up for you, and
  what forms do they take?
- How can you use the "surfing" practice to work with these
  edges?
- Which one of the other practices in this chapter would you like
  to try when challenging emotions triggered by uncertainty arise?

A MEDITATION ON SECURITY

One autumn, I went for a hike at one of my favorite places on the planet, Ghost Ranch, in Abiquiú, New Mexico. This is the land that Georgia O'Keeffe fell madly in love with, where she spent many years capturing the majesty and mystery of the earth and sky in her paintings.

I chose the Box Canyon Trail, one I hadn't been on for a few years. Since my last visit, tremendous summer monsoons and a magnitude of rain had caused flooding in the area. As I made my way through the twists and turns of the trail, I felt disoriented. Nothing was where I remembered it. Could this possibly be the same path I had been on before? My feet had memorized a way through the canyon, but it wasn't this one! I looked for familiar forks in the trail and landmarks, but everything was different.

When I arrived at the stream that flows through the center of the canyon, I saw uprooted trees everywhere. Some of these trees were lodged in places that had been the original trail, now blocked and entirely rerouted. The roots of these upside-down trees had caught all kinds of natural debris: rocks, feathers, leaves, sand.

I sat down on a boulder, noticing how unsettled I felt. There between the high canyon walls, I looked up and near the very top of the northern wall I saw a rock column that I remembered from before, standing like a sentry over this disarray. I realized how much I count on something as seemingly solid as the earth to be unchanging. Yet here I was, in a landscape of upheaval.

Everything and anything can change, in any moment. We know this intellectually but it's a different story when our body experiences it. Those who have experienced serious illness and who have been touched by death know this truth intimately. When I asked Jami Sieber what helped her deal with the uncertainty of her path as a musician, especially earlier in her career, she told me,

> *I was very sick when I was fourteen and almost died. I experienced a great deal of fear, and yet I survived. That became the basis of how I lived after that. There was something about facing death and giving in to that possibility that my illness would limit my ability to speak or do other things. It became my teacher, and the basis of how I find courage in my life. It took me years to recognize that gift. I really see it now. That's my guide, and that also led me to healing work. I saw what human touch and human presence can do, the presence of heart.*

Katya Lesher had a similar story:

> *Having been diagnosed with cancer myself, and having been around death and dying and illness, I know that anybody's life can change in an instant.*
>
> *I feel like we've been convinced that if we do certain things in a certain way, we'll be secure, and it's not true. People lose their jobs every single day, or have an accident or illness that prevents them from doing their jobs. None of it is certain. Just recognizing this is freeing to me. We have an out breath, and that may be our last out breath. But then we have another one, and it's like "Yay, what can I do in this moment?" That's what we have, each moment.*

We have this idea that we can count on things happening in a certain way if we do certain things. We think if we are a reliable, hard worker, we will be rewarded. The idea of "Security" traps and deadens us more than we realize. I don't mean to flippantly dismiss your concerns but I do want you to realize that you may have less security than you think with your current job—or anything. The truth is that everything is impermanent. Our innate need to feel safe and in control is in direct conflict with the truth of nature: everything changes. There is no guarantee that something won't happen that results in big changes in your current work situation, and this is out of your control (despite the illusion of control that we often hang on to).

Eve Ensler, the author of *The Vagina Monologues* and founder of One Billion Rising, brings this point home in a powerful way:

> *In fact, security is essentially elusive, impossible. We all die. We all get sick. We all get old. People leave us. People surprise us. People change us. Nothing is secure. And this is the good news. But only if you are not seeking security as the point of your life.... I am proposing that we reconceive the dream. That we consider what would happen if security were not the point of our existence. That we find freedom, aliveness, and power not from what contains, locates, or protects us but from what dissolves, reveals, and expands us.* [13]

When your life is guided by your Core Intention rather than by other people's expectations, the rewards are great. All that's required is the courage to let go of the myth of security, and the openness to venture into "unanswered wonder" as Jami beautifully describes it.

CHAPTER 8 Key 5: Think Big and Make the Most of Your Resources

There is nothing enlightened about shrinking so that other people won't feel insecure around you...As we let our own light shine, we unconsciously give other people permission to do the same. As we are liberated from our own fear, our presence automatically liberates others.

—Marianne Williamson

If you have difficulty allowing yourself to imagine all the possibilities for a Liberation-Based Livelihood, this Key will give your visioning and empowerment muscles a workout. Key 5 helps you to think big and realize that you have the power to make your dreams become a reality, and you can generate the resources needed to do this.

This Key is the one that's the most challenging for me. I have been well trained in thinking small. As a young girl, my mom's career guidance to me was. *You can be anything you want when you grow up, but make sure you know how to type and take shorthand so if things don't work out you can fall back on being a secretary.*

My mom was looking out for me and gave this advice out of love, I'm certain of that. Her own perspective was indelibly informed by growing up as a first-generation daughter of an Eastern European immigrant family during the Great Depression, and it made a lot of sense to have this "fall back" strategy as a way to survive those tough economic times.

But that guidance had a chilling effect on my own ability to imagine what was possible for my livelihood and my life. I learned how to squash all my passions. *Writer? Forget it, no one makes money that way. Geologist? I'm not smart enough. Big league baseball player? Nah … impossible.* (The gender factor blocked that route as well.)

So I hedged my bets and played it safe with my first career by entering into the helping professions. At every career turn since, that phrase echoed inside me: "If it doesn't work out ..." with the implicit prediction that it probably wouldn't. The other phrase that has reverberated through me is, "I can't do _____ because I don't have enough money."

Do either or both of those phrases feel familiar to you?

One of the most pivotal experiences in transforming this pattern was serving as executive director of a nonprofit organization based in the San Francisco Bay Area. "Being an executive director" was not on my list of career goals. It came about because I was on the board of this organization as it was going through a particularly difficult time, and I was drafted into the position to help stabilize things.

I have a fairly introverted personality—although I describe myself as a gregarious introvert—and if you had to pin me down to any one identity, it would be "writer." It surely would not be "executive director," a leadership position that some might say is better suited to extroverts. I thought long and hard before accepting the request to take the position, knowing it would require a huge stretch outside my comfort zone.

Yet I made it through three years of directing, leading, managing, budgeting, fundraising, and schmoozing with quite a bit of success. If something in my organization's vision was crying out to be manifested—like a new project that would benefit many people—I began to realize that I had it in my power to acquire the resources needed to put it into place. I learned to "think big," to get the organization's supporters excited about the project, and to create a fundraising campaign to get it off the ground. For someone like me who was taught early on to limit my possibilities, this was truly liberating.

By the time my term ended, I was very proud of what the organization had accomplished under my leadership, and realized that something inside me had transformed in this process of stretching myself. I was more than ready to go back to a quieter way of living, but I'd learned something invaluable: the skills that I had honed in that position could serve me in other areas. In essence, I could become the executive director of my own life.

That experience helped me to shift my guiding question from "What happens if this doesn't work out?" to other, more exciting questions, such as these:

- "What happens if it *does* work out?"
- "What if it works out in a way I didn't expect but is equally and maybe even more fulfilling?"

- "What resources do I need to make this work out? How can I find them?"

WHAT'S YOUR RELATIONSHIP WITH THIS KEY?

Ask yourself the following questions to assess your current relationship with this key:

- What's your biggest vision for work that matters? In your wildest imagination, what would a Liberation-Based Livelihood look like for you?
- What would it take to make that vision become reality? What kinds of resources would you need?
- How easy or difficult is it for you to answer these questions, or even think about them?

The "think big" part of this Key is not intended to imply that the only jobs, careers, or projects that matter are the ones that make a lot of money and impact large numbers of people. You can do small-scale things guided by your Core Intention and do them beautifully, even if only one other person (or creature) benefits from them.

"Think big" in this context refers to breaking out of your self-imposed cage of underestimating what's possible, of thinking you don't have enough of what you need. How often do we get attached to the very smallest version of ourselves when something more magnificent is longing to come through? Jess Huffman, a Fall in Love with Your Work participant and life coach from Canada, notes: "You can't learn to think big if you are in love with thinking small."

I believe that all of us have a natural brilliance that is yearning to come out and be expressed in the daily activities of our life, including our work. This spark longs to be seen by others not in a superficial, attention-getting way, but in the most authentic way possible. Buddhists call this "Buddha-nature," our awakened self. It is luminous and radiant, and it is a gift we give to others. It is our original nature before a whole lot of internal and external crap gets piled on it. That luminosity is there in all of us, but we often forget it or lose our way.

A number of factors can cut us off from this inherent brilliance. Let's look at some of these in more detail.

WE HAVE A FEAR OF STANDING OUT

It's easier to stay small and invisible. We stay "safe" that way. When you step fully into your power and presence, you become more visible and therefore a more likely target for other people's criticisms as well as projections.

WE HAVE RESISTANCE TO RECEIVING

When we take a chance and let our true nature shine, we may feel uncomfortable receiving the love and appreciation that come back to us. We may not realize that giving and receiving are two sides of the same coin. When we step fully into our deepest selves, we are actually giving something to others.

Consider the people who inspired you early in your life. It's likely they made such an impact on you because they fully embraced their gifts and shared them with others, including you, in an unfettered way. They didn't play small.

There's even research to back this up. In a Massachusetts Institute of Technology (MIT) study of the West Bengal region of India, where quotas for female politicians in local governments have been in place since 1993, researchers surveyed families in nearly five hundred villages about their attitudes on education and achievement. They compared the responses to those of villages without any women in political leadership roles. In the areas where women had been in government, they found that teenage girls set higher goals for themselves and parents were more likely to have ambitious goals for their daughters

Esther Duflo, MIT economist and coauthor of the study, said, "We think this is due to a role-model effect: Seeing women in charge persuaded parents and teens that women can run things, and increased their ambitions. Changing perceptions and giving hope can have an impact on reality." [14]

THERE ARE SOCIAL AND CULTURAL REASONS FOR BACKING OFF FROM OUR BRILLIANCE

Women and people in other marginalized groups have received a lifetime of messages about being "less than" and staying in "your place." We may come to believe these messages, based on misinformation and stereotypes. It takes great effort to identify and overcome them.

This dynamic is a form of internalized oppression, and it can impact individuals as well as groups that share the same cultural background. Recently I gave a presentation to an audience that included a number of older white males with a background in quantitative sciences and business. I noticed my body tense up and my insecurities start to rise. I hesitated and was ready to censor myself, as I fell into the trap of seeing my presentation through their eyes: "I need to add more statistics.... This may be too touchy-feely for them...."

These were messages that I had internalized based on our society's tendency to value "hard" sciences such as neuroscience and biology over social sciences, and to consider ways of knowing often associated with men (logic, quantitative data, statistics) as more legitimate than ways of knowing associated with women (intuition, art, storytelling, relating our personal experiences).[15] Fortunately, I was able to use the same basic mindfulness practice that I shared earlier as a way to understand what was going on and to reconnect with my innate strength and confidence. When I became cognizant of how my own internalized oppression around gender was showing up, I reminded myself that I had a unique perspective to offer, one grounded in my training as a cultural anthropologist, and that this approach was as valid as any other. I put my big-girl panties on and let the chips fall where they may. While some of those men may have been critical of my presentation, I didn't let it get to me. Most of the folks in the audience came up afterward and said they appreciated it and learned a lot, and I felt great that I didn't give my power away in order to appease the dominant paradigm and please everyone.

The way to break free from internalized oppression is to acknowledge its existence and to listen to the stories of other people in our cultural group (women, people of color, people with different physical/mental abilities, etc.) so we can begin to understand how our experience is a product of our socialization, not our own weakness or "fault." By doing so, we remove the barriers to expressing our particular kind of intelligence and wisdom. We can practice claiming our own vision and voice, and letting them shine brightly.

WE ARE OVERLY ATTACHED TO OUTCOMES

We may have a rigid set of expectations about what we want to see happen in ourselves and in others. While intentions are essential, when they get reified into attachment, we create suffering for ourselves and others, and we block the flow of that shining true nature. When we stay true to an intention but are willing to be flexible about how we get there, we create more possibilities for liberation.

You'll know that you're caught in the "thinking small" trap if the following lines run through your head, which all start with: "I can't do this because ..."

- I don't have enough money.
- I don't have the skills.
- I'm not the kind of person who could do that.
- This doesn't fit into the kind of work I've done in my past ... it will look weird on my résumé.
- There are already too many (coaches, artists, massage therapists, rattlesnake wranglers, etc., fill in the blank) out there. I can't compete with that.

What happens when you free yourself from this cage of not-enoughness and allow yourself to imagine what your beautiful livelihood would look and feel like? Here are some examples from Fall in Love with Your Work graduates:

- Katya imagined "a place that would combine working space for my art along with a space where people come in for creative expression. I'd love to create a space where people can come and do healing work."
- Genevieve's vision also involved physical space. She pictured an eco-friendly home and a light-filled barn where she and her team would create photography and documentary film projects for progressive organizations. "Community" was a key ingredient in her vision, which included coworking spaces, workshops based on a connection to the land and self, and residencies for writers and artists.
- Leslie's dream was located at a more subtle level. She was committed to her core belief that "life is good and it's meant to be enjoyed." She recognized that it wouldn't always be easy or fun, "but in a deep way life is meant to be joyful." Holding that vision as her North Star has guided Leslie's choices around work and life.

I want to say a word about resistance, which can kick in here perhaps more than in any other Key. Audre Lorde once said, "We have been raised to fear the yes within ourselves, our deepest cravings." A friend of mine, Nathalie Rodriguez, shared the following piece of wisdom near the start of her time in graduate school to study clinical social work and to pursue her vision:

So it turns out that actually answering your deepest calling (in my case to be of service to folks who are suffering as they face illness and death and to create new health systems that are whole, inclusive, and supportive) requires you to engage with all of the resistance that emerges as you answer that calling.

Some of the symptoms of this resistance may include:

- *sabotaging your efforts*
- *disengaging (mentally, emotionally, physically)*
- *"failing"*
- *fighting with the people you love*
- *fighting with yourself*
- *experiencing deep exhaustion*
- *numbing/bypassing your feelings of inadequacy, fear, anxiety*
- *eating too much or too little*
- *entertaining a "fuck it, this will never change" attitude about the system you want to dismantle*
- *not asking for help*
- *refusing to be vulnerable and admit your limitations*
- *believing that you are a victim of your calling/circumstances/ graduate program, etc.*

I have experienced all of these symptoms in the past few weeks. I naively thought that all of my years of inner work, excellent self-care, and spiritual practices would somehow make me immune to the struggle and emotional labor of navigating resistance that are often necessary to answer a deep calling.

I want to honor and normalize the very real struggles that we must face when we say yes to becoming who we really are. To do this, first we have to be brave enough to admit that we may not be fully on board with our becoming. Resistance can be useful. It can be the fertilizer that shows us where we are stuck and all the ways that we believe we are not worthy or too small to do the work we were born to do.

If you find yourself in the fertile field of resistance while working through this Key, this might be a good time to take another look at chapter 3 and ask yourself which of the three building blocks of transformation (Returning to This Very Moment, Leveraging Adversity, Staying the Course) would be helpful to you at this stage of the process.

ON RESOURCES ...

"Thinking small" can take the form of overlooking or minimizing the resources available to us. We may think of resources as synonymous with money, but sometimes what's most needed to reach your livelihood-related goal is something else—more of your time and creativity, or perhaps the support of friends and family. Our life experiences, skills, time, and perhaps most importantly, our community, are all part of our resources (more on that in Key 6, Build a Circle of Allies and Ask for Help). Key 5's call to think big invites us to think along a whole spectrum of resources, not just the financial kind.

Author of *The Soul of Money* and activist Lynne Twist is the very definition of a visionary; her perspective can enrich our view of "resources." For more than forty years, she has nurtured her vision of alleviating global poverty and hunger in tandem with supporting social justice and environmental sustainability. She cofounded the Pachamama Alliance to empower indigenous people of the Amazon rainforest to preserve their lands and culture, and also to educate and inspire people everywhere to bring forth a thriving, just, and sustainable world.

Through Lynne's teaching and writing, she helps people from all walks of life transform their relationship to money and other kinds of resources. One of Lynne's greatest teachings is that we have the capacity to shift our mind-set from scarcity to sufficiency:

> *When we turn our love and attention away from what we think we need to what we already have—financially, emotionally, physically, and spiritually—and nourish it, express it, and most importantly, share it, experiences of profound prosperity, wholeness, and sufficiency flood our lives.*[16]

KEY 5 PRACTICES
1. THE BIG IDEA JOURNAL

Create a space that is dedicated to your dreams and visions: a BIG IDEA journal, sketchbook, or even a collection of audio files. Ask yourself: If there were no limits, what is my dream for my work and life? Give yourself permission to disregard the laws of nature, financial constraints, and social and family expectations … let your imagination run wild. Perhaps you'd start a worldwide organization dedicated to protecting elephants; or maybe you'd be a concert pianist; maybe you'd be an astronaut; or you would travel the world and get paid for it. The sky's the limit.

You don't have to execute on any of these ideas—the practice here is simply to give them space. At some later point in time, you might find it useful to look at the content of this journal, and even if your ideas are outrageous, they may contain the seeds of something that actually is doable. Make it a habit to play in this journal at least once a month so you can exercise your visioning skills.

2. LINEAGE OF INSPIRATION

This practice helps you tap into your "lineage," people who have inspired you and who held a special place in your heart. These luminaries reflect something of our own greatness back to us, and help expand our sense of what's possible.

Make a list of the people you most deeply admire. You can include people who are currently in your life, those who have died, historical figures, or even mythical characters. My list, for example, has included Eleanor Roosevelt, Indiana Jones, and the Dalai Lama. (An odd combination I know. I am full of paradoxes!) All three were or are risk takers, willing to go against conventional wisdom because they trust their own instincts, and this is a quality I strive to cultivate in myself.

What are the qualities in them that you admire? How do you possess those qualities, even in nascent form? When you are facing a career challenge, you might want to ask yourself how one of your exemplars might face the situation. Write down your responses to these questions next to the name of each person on your list.

As you look at your own list, what are the qualities in these people that you admire? Look at your collage whenever you need to draw on inspiration from your spiritual/archetypal lineage.

3. APPRECIATING YOUR RESOURCES

Bring out your journal and take an inventory of your resources as they relate to your livelihood goals. You will be drawing on this list when we get to the Personal Mission Statement process in chapter 10 so keep it in a place for easy reference.

Don't limit the definition of "resources" to financial ones (although it's helpful to include that kind of asset if you have it). These questions will help you uncover resources you may not realize you have:

- What personal qualities do you possess? (e.g., I am a great listener, I am good at giving difficult feedback to people, I have a wicked sense of humor and can lighten the mood in any group, etc.)
- What skills do you have? (e.g., I can build a website, I can knit an incredible afghan, I'm a fantastic cook, etc.)

- What kind of time do you have to invest in learning new skills or experimenting with new forms of work?
- What kind of financial and material resources do you have to work with? Include savings accounts, retirement accounts if that's something you can draw on, housing.
- Who in your community of friends and colleagues can help you with career- and work-related goals? List all the supportive people that you know.
- What groups, organizations, or networks are you connected with that can help you move toward your work-related goals?
- What unique personal and professional experiences do you have that can help you move toward your next stage of livelihood?

You may find that this practice of listing your resources helps you to see new possibilities for your Liberation-Based Livelihood. It might even result in a new perspective on how all of your life experiences up until this point in time, which may have seemed so disparate, actually interweave and interconnect as it did for Yael.

As she took stock of her resources, Yael recognized a number of valuable nonfinancial assets that could support the creation of her dream early childhood program. In addition to the Waldorf teacher training she had done years earlier and a scholarship to do another training (in Hawai'i!) in a Waldorf "Lifeways" program that would give her a certificate in early childhood education, Yael also reflected on over four decades of her experience as a feminist activist, Zen mindfulness practitioner, mother of her own children, and her desire to support other parents of young children. She identified other threads that were interwoven throughout her lifetime:

- love of being in nature, and a lifelong practice of conservation and living lightly on the Earth;
- appreciation for simple beauty;
- deep commitment to cultivating community and being of service;
- cherishing time for silent meditation and being alone;
- treasuring the connection with her Jewish heritage and its rootedness in the cycles of the moon and the rhythms of the seasons.

Taking the long view, Yael could also see how music and storytelling, ritual and ceremony, crafting and creative expression have all played a consistent role in helping to delight and sustain her throughout her lifetime. All of these practices and "threads" became the foundation for establishing Kulanu, the Zen Jewish Waldorf preschool Yael created on her country property in northern California, and they continue to provide the framework and support for her daily work with the children in her care. "I'm living my dream!" she often says. Her days are filled with gratitude and amazement—that after a lifetime of dancing in so many different directions, and swimming in so many streams, she has managed to incorporate *all of them* not only in a way that enriches her life immeasurably, but also sustains her spiritually and financially.

EXPLORATION: 360-DEGREE SURVEY

Our friends and colleagues can often see things about ourselves that we can't, or see them in a different light that can help things click into place for us. That's exactly what this survey process is designed to do for you.

First, think of at least three friends and/or colleagues who you will invite to help you with this survey. The people you speak with should know you well enough to be familiar with your unique qualities and gifts. If they've interacted with you professionally, that's great, but it's not a requirement. It's good to include a diverse range of people in your survey: colleagues (past and current), supervisors, people that you've supervised, family members, and close friends. If you come up with more than three names, that's even better. An optimal number for this survey is between seven and ten people.

Once you've decided whom you'll include in your survey, here are the questions you'll ask them:

1. What do you know to be my unique strengths and gifts (personally or in my work)?
2. What do you value most about me and/or my work?
3. What kinds of challenges have I helped you to solve or meet in the past?
4. If you needed assistance in some area of your life or work, when would I be the first person you'd think of to ask for help? On what specific kinds of tasks or projects?

(e.g., to help me organize my files, to help me move through a period of grieving, to help me get in the habit of eating more nutritious foods…)

5. Can you think of any ways I could change how I do my work that would better reflect/use my talents?
6. How or in what ways have I inspired you in your own life?

If some of the questions don't make sense in your situation, feel free to adapt them in a way that feels right to you.

There are a few ways you can carry out this process:

1. Invite your interviewee to coffee and do the survey in person. This is often the most gratifying way to do the survey, both for you and the person you're speaking with. Who knows what will come from connecting or reconnecting?
2. Talk with a few of your interviewees together—kind of like a focus group.
3. Send the questions by email or set this up as an online survey so that you can reach people in faraway locations. This is probably the most efficient way to run this survey, and it has the advantage of collecting the responses in a digital file so you can save them for reference later. It's easy to set up a free account on SurveyMonkey (www.surveymonkey.com) for surveys of ten questions or less.
4. Combine any of the above. Do one or two in-person surveys, and the remainder via email.

However you do it, you'll get some very rich information and insights that will help you to recognize internal resources. Make sure you collect all of these responses in a place that's easy to find, as you'll be drawing on them when you craft your Personal Mission Statement in chapter 10.

You may feel tentative about doing this exercise, but please don't let that stop you. Most people consider it an honor to be invited to help and usually really enjoy the process. Many Fall in Love with Your Work course participants have been pleasantly surprised at what transpired through this exercise. Katya shared, "While I felt a bit shy and hesitant to put it out there, when I finally did, I was so grateful to hear from my friends and colleagues. What a beautiful gift it was to hear their perspective." Genevieve said, "I'm so glad I did it! To have people speak to the best in me helps me see it in myself, and make decisions from that place instead of a place of weakness."

INTEGRATING KEY 5

Find a quiet place. Sit down with the following questions and see what answers arise. Use your journal to write down your observations.

- What gets in the way of your natural brilliance being expressed?
- When you give yourself permission to "think big" about your work, what happens? How does it feel? What do you imagine?
- What resources have you been overlooking or taken for granted? How can they support you to create a Liberation-Based Livelihood?

A MEDITATION ON MANIFESTATION

Manifestation is the process of bringing our vision into reality. It's a word that often pops up in New Agey, self-indulgent contexts to serve as a code meaning "getting what I want no matter how self-serving, or ignorant of reality or others' needs it may be." For that reason I was suspicious of it for a long time. But I've come to realize that true manifestation is an essential component in a Liberation-Based Livelihood and it doesn't have to be selfish. We have to have some degree of faith that we can manifest our vision of work we love in order to make it really happen.

In recent years, I've surprised myself with my ability to conjure up things that I have wished for, including meaningful and sustainable work. I don't mean this in a magical thinking kind of way, though sometimes it can feel like that. It's more that as I've gotten clearer in understanding my Core Intention and how something relates to it (like financial stability, or a supportive partner), that thing soon appears in my life. It may not arrive in exactly the package I was expecting, but it shows up. It wasn't always like this. I remember feeling like it used to take years, if ever, to attain what I imagined.

How is it that manifestation sometimes happens so easily and other times we have to struggle with every ounce of might to birth something into the world? Philosopher David Spangler makes a helpful distinction between manifestation and its shallow twin, the Law of Attraction.[17] As Spangler notes, the problem with the Law of Attraction is that it tends to be a self-centered exercise in trying to get what we want, like lots of money, a beach home, or the perfect lover. (Is there a perfect lover? Have you found one?) It exists to the exclusion of other people.

Manifestation, on the other hand, asks the question, What kind of people/work/environment will help me to be able to offer my greatest gifts to the world? In contrast to the Law of Attraction, manifestation is all about the greater good, not our self-centered desires. Astrologer Rob Brezsny sums up the bighearted nature of this process quite well:

> You can have anything you want if you'll just ask for it in an unselfish way. The trick to making this work is to locate where your deepest ambition coincides with the greatest gift you have to give. Figure out exactly how the universe, by providing you with abundance, can improve the lot of everyone whose life you touch. Seek the fulfillment of your fondest desires in such a way that you become a fount of blessings.[18]

Through this process of manifestation we can see more clearly what's needed to help our light shine in the world, and then how to make a request for that ingredient. Which leads us into Key 6, in which we call for support from the people around us.

CHAPTER 9   Key 6: Build a Circle of Allies and Ask for Help

I am what I am because of who we all are.

—Definition of "Ubuntu," an African ethic of
interconnection, offered by Liberian peace activist
Leymah Gbowee

If you're feeling alone on your journey to a Liberation-Based Livelihood, this Key reminds you of the essential role that other people play in this process, and guides you in building a supportive circle of allies. These are people who will embody a more liberating way of working (and living), and by doing so, will expand your own sense of what's possible. These are people who are willing to share their resources to support you to succeed. If you find it challenging to reach out and ask for help, this Key also supports you to learn how to receive (and give).

In my early thirties, I ended my career as a mental health professional and moved to San Francisco for graduate school. As I got to know fellow students and other people in my new hometown, I realized I had never met so many folks who didn't have nine-to-five jobs. It wasn't because they were rich and didn't have to work. Most were just like me—students struggling to balance school and life, or if they weren't students, they were regular women and men without a trust fund or other treasure trove of money.

I was puzzled about how my new friends were able to survive this way. How could you pay the rent and buy groceries without a regular job? Having lived in other places that were more mainstream in regards to lifestyle and employment, this was all new to me, as I had worked a full-time job for many years and was just starting my graduate student life.

What I discovered was an "off-the-grid" approach to livelihood and life. Some of these folks did freelance work; others were engaged in time banks and bartered their skills. Some became house sitters and pet sitters for a free place to live or for money, or both. A few (including me) signed up to be medical research subjects at local universities. I still remember the asthma study I participated in when I had to pedal an indoor bike while smog-like air was pumped into a chamber. Ugh. But I picked up a sweet five hundred dollars over a few weeks, which was a great help in supporting my low-income grad student life.

"Resourceful" was another descriptor for my new friends, who had some very innovative ways of saving money. Some of them lived in cooperative housing situations to keep rent costs down. Many didn't own a car, instead they used public transportation or rode bikes. They shopped at thrift stores and yet still put together stylish wardrobes. A few made a practice of dumpster diving to obtain furniture for their apartments, and sometimes even food. As one told me, you have no idea of the delicacies you can find in the trash!

These people had stepped off the socially proscribed treadmill of working fulltime for someone else, often in a job you didn't like, and doing that until you are at least sixty years old, at which point you think you can relax. Except you probably won't because you're worried you haven't saved enough money in your retirement account.

In contrast, these folks were passionate about their work and had figured out how to do it in a place with a high cost of living. Some might call them bohemians or dropouts, but they were actually highly disciplined, principled people. Following in the noble footsteps of Henry David Thoreau and Mohandas Gandhi, they practiced reducing their consumption of consumer goods, sharing resources, and simplifying their life so they could focus on what was most important to them. They had changed the definition of "how much is enough." Watching them gave me the inspiration and courage to see my work and life in a new way.

Key 6, Build a Circle of Allies and Ask for Help, is an extension of Key 5, in which we learned how to identify and appreciate many different kinds of resources. In this Key, we focus on the most precious resource of all: the people in your life.

WHAT'S YOUR RELATIONSHIP WITH THIS KEY?

Ask yourself the following questions to assess your current relationship with this key:

- Think about your current circle of friends and other acquaintances. How happy are they with their work? How happy are they in their life?
- When you share your ideas about changes you want to make in your professional life, what level of support do you receive from these people? Do they affirm your aspirations? Or do they try to discourage you?
- How easy or difficult is it for you to ask for what you need? When you consider approaching someone for help or assistance, what kinds of feelings and thoughts do you notice arising in you?

I intentionally chose the word "allies" for this Key rather than "friends," though allies can of course include your friends. However, I have a more specific meaning in mind. The word "ally" shares the same etymological root as "alloy"—a combination of two or more metallic elements that results in a material with greater strength and stronger resistance to corrosion. Both words come from the Latin *alligare*, which means "to bind together." Like an alloy, allies make each other stronger. An ally is someone who joins with another person or group to offer support. This support can take many forms: encouragement, connections to pivotal people, financial means, mentorship, training, and more.

This process of building a circle of allies has some overlap with the concept of networking, but it goes deeper than that. Networking usually takes the form of going to countless "networking events," exchanging business cards, and developing rather superficial relationships. It's easy to go into networking from the perspective of what you can *get* from it. This Key teaches us to nurture genuine relationships for the long-term, and to *give* as much as we receive.

An ally may be someone you don't know in a social context but you feel a resonance with in your workplace or another setting. These are people who want to see you fulfill your vision of a Liberation-Based Livelihood, and are willing to offer their resources to help you do that. Ally also implies that there is reciprocity in the relationship, that you would do the same for them. You have a shared commitment to each other's success. Allies are people who have created work that matters (or are in the process of creating it), and because they know how deeply fulfilling that is, they want to help others.

BUILDING YOUR CIRCLE AND THE POWER OF INFLUENCE

There is a simple yet powerful truth you'll discover on your journey to create a Liberation-Based Livelihood: you will only be as happy with your life and successful in your work as the people that you surround yourself with.

Social influence is a field of psychology that explores how other people affect our emotions, opinions, and behaviors. One of the most comprehensive studies in this area, published in the *New England Journal of Medicine* in 2007, followed the health habits of more than twelve thousand people for thirty-two years in conjunction with their social networks. Here's what researchers found:

- An individual's chances of becoming obese increased by 57 percent when that person's friend became obese.
- When two people considered themselves mutually close friends, the likelihood of one becoming obese after the other skyrocketed to 171 percent.
- This same pattern was evident between married partners and siblings, though to a lesser degree.[19]

These findings suggest that once a person becomes obese, it becomes more socially acceptable for those close to him or her to gain weight as well. One of the authors of the study, Nicholas Christakis, said,

> *What spreads is an idea. As people around you gain weight, your attitudes about what constitutes an acceptable body size changes, and you might follow suit and emulate that body size. It may cross some kind of threshold, and you can see an epidemic take off. Once it starts, it's hard to stop it. It can spread like wildfire.*[20]

In other words, our beliefs and behaviors are like a social contagion. Fortunately, the study found that the opposite was true as well. When a friend started practicing healthier habits and lost weight, the other friend was more likely to do the same.

When I think about the viral positive impact that people can have on each other, I immediately think of my friend and mentor Roshi Joan Halifax and her groundbreaking work with caregivers and others. Those who care for the chronically ill, whether they are professionals or family members, face many challenges ranging from burnout to secondary trauma to moral distress (stress that occurs when you know the "right" thing to do, but you work in an institution that makes it difficult or impossible to do that thing). It can be easy to go to a place of "sinking mind," as Roshi calls it, and be consumed with despair. When that happens, the caregiver's mental state can negatively impact the person whom she or he is caring for. Through a practice she developed called G.R.A.C.E., Roshi supports caregivers to cultivate altruistic and prosocial mental qualities such as compassion and resilience. This greatly enhances their capacity to be with another person who is in distress. (G.R.A.C.E. stands for the five elements at the heart of the process: gathering attention, recalling intention, attuning to self and other, considering what will serve, and engaging, enacting, ending. You can learn more about G.R.A.C.E. at www.upaya.org.)

I got a chance to see this dynamic in action when I traveled with Roshi on a month-long trek to Mount Kailash in Tibet in 1999. The journey was very difficult at times, as our group faced harsh weather and trail conditions. On one particular day, we received news that a major storm was coming our way, making it potentially dangerous to navigate a treacherous Himalayan mountain pass. One person went into a panic, with several others following suit. Soon a small subset of our group wanted to find a way to rent a helicopter rather than traverse the pass.

Roshi brought us all together and invited us to sit in meditation as a group and settle our minds. We then engaged in a mindful discussion about our options. The fear and anxiety that had been spreading through the group soon dissipated, and we made a calm and informed decision to go ahead with the hike through the pass, renewing our commitment to take care of each other on the way. It was a wonderful teaching on how we condition one another, and the importance of grounding ourselves so that we can make a positive rather than negative impact on each other.

When I think about the powerful role of influence in the context of creating a Liberation-Based Livelihood, what's clear to me is this: be on the lookout for people who are where you want to be, in terms of their relationship with work. Watch for those who are passionate about what they do for a living and genuinely happy in their professional life. Invite them into your life with more frequency.

Lyndon's experience reinforces this point:

The company you keep is very important. Ten years ago I had a whole different set of social friends. Now I hang out with a lot of diverse people who are artists, really creative and energetic people. Those kinds of people motivate me, they encourage me. When I had the idea to start a new business of making beard oil, people were really excited about it. Whether it's online, or in town, find people you can go to and get support for your ideas.

Remember Key 2 (Value Your Gifts and Time)? This comes into play here. Value yourself and your aspiration enough to surround yourself only with people who embody right livelihood. Start making a list of potential allies. These might be people already in your circle: friends, family members, coworkers, mentors. They might be people you've noticed online. Whoever they are, this is a great time to start or deepen relationships with them. The more that you have the foundation of an authentic and caring relationship in place, the more natural it will be to ask for their support when the time feels right.

You may also want to consider bringing someone into your life whose sole purpose is to support you to create a Liberation-Based Livelihood, such as a life or business coach. Leslie took this route when she started her business, Threads of Awakening:

For me, a really important part of having a business coach was having somebody who believed that it was possible for me to create my business. My coach offered an unquestioning, constant faith that I could do it. That has kept me willing to find a way to do it, even when I thought it was impossible.

If you decide that you want to work with a coach, how do you go about choosing one? Their level of certification is not always the most relevant factor. It's important to find someone with whom you feel a basic level of trust. Most life and business coaches will offer a complimentary exploration session so that you can ask questions about their approach and get a sense of how it might be to work with them. Take full advantage of this, and remember this will require an investment of your time and money so make sure you feel good about entering into a relationship with this person. An increasing number of coaches (including myself) are grounded in a mindfulness-based perspective, which can be helpful if that resonates with you. (And if you've gotten this far in the book, I'd say the answer is "yes" to that one!)

It's equally important to have the discipline to say "no" to anyone who dismisses your vision of doing work that you love or focuses on all the reasons why it can't happen. The less you allow that kind of negative influence into your life, the greater your own progress toward a Liberation-Based Livelihood will be. This doesn't mean there's no room for constructive criticism. But there's a huge difference between people who want to support you to become the biggest version of yourself and those who are stuck in seeing only smallness in themselves and you.

Transformative initiatives tend to create their own momentum, and you may find that the more you set your intention to surround yourself with supportive and inspiring people, the less room there is for relationships that aren't generative. Martha, a Fall in Love with Your Work course graduate, found this to be true:

> Over the past couple of years, I have made a lot more space for the people I respect and love and who respect and love me back—the best quid pro quo. During that time I have found that other people have fallen away, or those that are still in my life don't get to me as much as they did before. I never want to close myself off, but now I try to fill my time with loving, kind people, instead of being bogged down by people who would happily take from me until there was nothing left. Boundaries are my new best friend.

HOW TO ASK FOR HELP

Once you've begun to build this circle of allies, don't be afraid to ask them for help. Invite them to tea—literally, if they're in your geographic area, or virtually if you've connected online. Share your vision with them. Invite their ideas and suggestions for resources. Ask what you can do for *them*, so it's a mutually beneficial relationship.

This act of asking may push you up against your comfort zone. You already got a chance to begin practicing this with the 360-Degree Survey when you asked people for their time and their honest perspective of your gifts and skills. If you resist the idea of approaching someone with a request for support, please jump ahead to the "Meditation on Giving and Receiving" at the end of this chapter, and then come back to this section.

Musician Amanda Palmer (of the Dresden Dolls) learned a lot about asking for help when she worked as a "living statue" after graduating from college. Every day she would head out to the city streets and stand on a milk crate as the "Eight-Foot Bride." When someone walked by and handed her money, she would offer them a flower and eye contact. Some of her encounters with passersby were profound, particularly with lonely people who may not have had meaningful contact with anyone else.

Palmer continued the practice of asking as she toured with her band, inviting local musicians and artists to pass a hat, gratefully receiving home-cooked food from fans, and using Twitter to ask for places to stay along the tour route. As her band became more popular, she decided to leave her record label and independently produce her music. Once again, she needed the help of her fans to make this happen. In one of the most successful crowdfunding campaigns ever, Palmer surpassed her original goal of $100,000 and ended up raising nearly $1.2 million from nearly 25,000 people.

In her book, *The Art of Asking: How I Learned to Stop Worrying and Let People Help,* Palmer writes:

> *Often it is our own sense that we are undeserving of help that has immobilized us. Whether it's in the arts, at work, or in our relationships, we often resist asking not only because we're afraid of rejection but also because we don't even think we deserve what we're asking for.*

Palmer went on to develop a generosity-based business model out of the relationships she built with her fans. Her biggest discovery during her years of street performance? People are actually *eager* to pay you for your work when it means something special to them.

Jami Sieber had a similar experience, and recounted her story of receiving help:

> *I was moving toward making* Hidden Sky, *my CD for the elephants. I was still working as a nurse, though very rarely. A friend of mine said, "I have a friend who has money. I want to connect her with you as I believe she will support your dream and enable you to quit your nursing job and really dive into this project and make it happen. I bet this CD is going to be what will help you take off in your career."*
>
> *And it was. It gave me my voice too. I discovered I really had something to say with* Hidden Sky. *This generous woman gave me forty thousand dollars to make the CD and to live for eight months so I could create the CD. This enabled me to claim the music as being this deeper statement which became more of a healing force.*
>
> *I have found people love to help. We love to support each other, we are wired to do that. I have noticed that people often feel a loss*

*when they don't have a clear way to give. It's so natural for us to
wonder, "How do I get connected with things that have meaning,
with friends who are doing those things? How can I support them,
how can I show up?"*

I have had to reckon with my own resistance to asking for help. At
times I've worried that I might be imposing on the other person. I've
found that keeping my focus on building a relationship based on common values and interests is what makes it possible to request support in
a heartfelt way

When I first started my website, *The Liberated Life Project*, as a platform for my writing, I kept an eye out for other bloggers who were
coming from a similar perspective, weaving together spirituality and
social change. I came across Marianne Elliott, a New Zealand-based
author of a wonderful book called *Zen Under Fire*. I learned that Marianne was quite active on Twitter so I started to share some of her tweets.
She noticed and sent me a note of appreciation.

Some months later, I found out she was coming to New Mexico to
teach yoga at a retreat in Taos. I wrote to her to ask if she'd like to
get together, and much to my delighted surprise, Marianne said yes.
It turned out she needed a ride from Santa Fe to the airport in Albu-
querque, so I offered to drive her. On our hour-long journey we had
a wonderful connection and a wide-ranging conversation. Marianne
shared freely with me about the online courses she created, and I learned
a great deal from her that helped me improve my own online offerings
and business model. Since that visit, we've continued to help promote
each other's programs and Marianne wrote a guest post for my blog
about yoga that significantly increased my readership.

That's the kind of mutually beneficial and deeply enjoyable relationship that can happen when you set your intention to build your circle of
allies in an authentic way.

KEY 6 PRACTICES
1. GRATITUDE
All genuine relationships are grounded in gratitude. As you build
your circle of allies, reach out to those who have already been a
supportive influence in your life and find a way to thank them.
Call them, send an email, or take them out to lunch. Extra points
if you do it the old-fashioned way: send a beautiful thank you card
by snail mail.

Whatever method you choose for reaching out, be very specific as you express your gratitude. Let the other person know exactly what it was they did for you or said to you, and how it has made a difference in your life.

2. SAY GOODBYE TO TOXIC RELATIONSHIPS

As you are in this process of creating a new story for the kind of work you do and how you do it, consider who in your life might be a toxic influence. Perhaps this is someone who is deeply embedded in the paradigm of work as something to be tolerated but not enjoyed. Or perhaps it is someone whose own worries about money and security are so dominant that they aren't able to imagine a livelihood that is based on meaning and purpose.

Pay attention to what goes on in your body when you're in the presence of those people. If you feel yourself constricting and having a sense of dread as you interact with them, that's a good clue that this is a toxic relationship.

When you identify someone whose messages about work have a strong negative impact on you, limit the amount of time you spend with that person. In some cases, you may want to end the relationship altogether. If it's not possible to either limit the time or end the relationship (as might be true for family members), practice setting boundaries around the kind of input they give you. You might try saying, "I appreciate that you care about me, but that kind of feedback is not helpful right now." Or, "I understand that's been your experience. It's really important to me to hold a vision for a different kind of reality for the work I do." What other responses can you imagine will be effective in holding your ground while continuing to maintain the relationship?

You can even role-play these kinds of conversations with a supportive friend or life coach so that you practice staying centered in your strength and confidence when interacting with someone who is coming from a negative perspective.

3. ASK FOR HELP

If you've taken time to build your circle of allies with intention, and if you've carefully nurtured your relationships with them, the practice of asking for help will feel more natural and less contrived. It is a practice! The more you do it, the better you'll get at it. There are also certain elements that you can cultivate to help the practice flow and bring about the most positive results:

Be Specific

Take time to get clear on exactly what you need to move you closer to a Liberation-Based Livelihood. Perhaps you are looking for an introduction to someone inside a company or business that has a mission very closely aligned with your own Core Intention. Or maybe you could benefit from learning about resources that will help you develop a certain set of skills. You might be seeking a job or freelance project to bring in some income. Maybe you are in need of emotional support and cheerleading to get you through a challenging time in your professional life.

Your list of needs might be diverse and long. That's okay, but it's usually best to focus on just one need at a time as you meet with your ally.

Be Skillful

My friend Roshi Joan Halifax chose to call her organization Upaya Zen Center, after the Sanskrit word *upaya*, which can be translated as "skillful means." This is a concept that recognizes that there is no one-size-fits-all solution, and we must find what works best given our unique situation.

As you consider what you need, what's the most appropriate way to ask? Who does it make sense to have a conversation with, based on their background and connections? What form might be most useful for making this request? Possibilities could include getting together in person with an individual, gathering a group of friends together in a virtual circle like a Skype call, or casting the net wider and making your request on Facebook or another social media channel.

Over the past couple of years, I've been making a practice of what I call "treasure hunting." When I've hit some dry patches in my business and need to generate income, I send a letter to a select group of my allies—those who in the past were very encouraging of my work, and who let me know they'd be happy to help if I ever needed it. In this letter, I'm very specific about what I have to offer (communication and fundraising skills, community building, writing, qualitative research) and what I am looking for in terms of work. I've also posted a shorter version on Facebook in order to cast a wider net. Some wonderful clients and projects have come through from this approach. I've included my own example of a "Treasure Hunting" letter in the Appendix, which you can adapt for your use. You'll notice that I list not only my skills, but also the qualities that make me valuable in a professional setting. Check back on your responses to the "Recognize Your Worth" practice in Key 2 to remind yourself what makes you so invaluable, and include this in your letter.

Be Bold

When you have this conversation with an ally, you may be tempted to disguise your request behind a wall of apologies ("I'm so sorry to take your time! I know you are busy, and you probably aren't able to do this any way, but I thought I'd try ..."), or to make it as small as possible. Don't water down what you're asking for. Remember, the other person can always say no—and you can make it clear to them that's an acceptable response. It's their responsibility to know what they can and can't offer; it's not up to you to decide that ahead of time on their behalf.

In her book *Stop Playing Safe*, Australian author and coach Margie Warrell writes, "Think about what your ideal outcome would be and then confidently, courageously, ask for it. Not in an entitled way. Not in an aggressive way. But in a way that conveys that you know your worth." You may want to review what you learned about yourself in Key 2, Value Your Gifts and Your Time, and bring those insights into this conversation.

Be Gracious

Recognize that the other person is already giving you their time and attention in this process. Express your sincere appreciation, and ask what you can do for them.

INTEGRATING KEY 6

Find a quiet place. Sit down with the following questions and see what answers arise. Use your journal to write down your observations.

- As you think about your circle of current friends, who is the most encouraging of your vision for work that matters? How can you invite them to be more present in your life?
- Are there new friendships and professional relationships you'd like to cultivate with people who embody Liberation-Based Livelihood? How can you take the first step toward doing that?
- What is one livelihood-related request that you'd like to practice making with someone in your circle of allies?

A MEDITATION ON GIVING AND RECEIVING

During longer Zen Buddhist retreats, participants eat their meals inside the zendo (meditation hall) in a practice called *oryoki*. Oryoki, from a Japanese word that means "just enough," is a beautiful and intricate ceremony with very specific protocols for how one receives the food being offered. The main point of the practice is to realize that "giver, receiver, and gift" are inseparable. In doing this practice, we begin to learn how to give from a full heart, without attachment, and how to receive with grace and gratitude.

In an oryoki ceremony, servers kneel down in front of each person and carefully spoon ladles of rice, soup, or whatever might be in their container into the bowls of the meditator. Once everyone has been served, meditators are invited to consider the source of these foods and offer gratitude in the form of a bow.

Taking part in oryoki ceremonies over many years has helped me to understand giving and receiving in a nontransactional way. So often we give something with an expectation that we'll get something back, whether that's a material object, prestige, respect, or even love. This kind of quid pro quo feels forced and awkward, and gets exhausting. It is one of the reasons why many people shy away from asking for help.

But what if we look at giving and receiving in another way. If we understand that we live in an *interdependent world*, to use Thich Nhat Hanh's phrase we see how we need each other to survive and thrive. We offer people a gift when we invite them to help us, in a genuine way that is based on relationship rather than transaction.

Think about a time when you gave something to an individual or group and it felt really great. You actually couldn't wait to offer your money, time, or expertise. What was it that made the difference? Why did that act of giving feel like a joy rather than an obligation or imposition?

My guess is that first of all you felt an affinity with the person doing the asking—even if you didn't know them well. Maybe they reminded you of a younger version of yourself. Second, that act of giving connected you with the asker in an intimate way, and we live in a society that is starved for true intimacy. Finally, your own joy may have increased as you saw the recipient of your gift be able to do something they couldn't do without your help.

I invite you to consider all this as you notice any resistance that may arise as you consider asking for help. What if, in asking another person for help, you are actually *offering* a gift to them? How might this awareness change your story around work?

PART III
Navigational Tools

On this journey that we've shared together so far, we've spent a lot of time on the internal dimension of transformation. The 6 Keys are the portal to knowing yourself better, understanding your strengths and the resources you have to draw on, and learning what internal barriers stand in the way of your Liberation-Based Livelihood.

Now it's time to turn to the external dimension of change. The navigational tools in this part of the book are intended to help you take practical actions so that you can love your work, whatever that looks like for you, and sustain yourself financially and in other ways.

This doesn't mean that you're finished with the 6 Keys, though. This internal work will be the basis of every action you take. If you find yourself getting stuck, consider which of the Keys could help you and which may be in need of more deepening and development.

For example, if you become clear that it's time to leave your job but you're unable to actually give notice to your boss or develop a plan for what comes next, spend some time reflecting on your relationship to Key 3 (Break Through Inertia and Take Action) and Key 4 (Make Friends with Uncertainty). Perhaps you've discovered that you love to work with kids through art, and you have the beginnings of a dream to develop this into a livelihood. But you freeze up because it seems impossible. If that's the case, revisit Key 5 (Think Big and Make the Most of Your Resources) and engage again with the practices that will develop that quality within you.

When you take part in this ongoing dance between the inner and outer aspects of change, you'll be amazed at how you can move through obstacles that may have previously seemed insurmountable.

CHAPTER 10   Craft Your Personal Mission Statement

Nonprofit organizations and businesses use mission statements to focus their efforts, to communicate their purpose to others, and to help them discern when to say "yes" and "no." This enables them to make the best use of their resources. In the same way, your Personal Mission Statement will be a powerful vehicle to carry you toward work you love with much greater momentum. Think of it like your magic broom—you won't get very far without it and you can't imagine the places you'll go with it.

A well-crafted Personal Mission Statement can help you:

- decide if a potential job is a good fit for you,
- set the stage for an entrepreneurial adventure,
- understand your current work in a new light, and
- connect it to your Core Intention (which makes all the difference in job satisfaction).

Most importantly, your mission statement gives you a blueprint through which you can design a life and livelihood that is a true expression of who you are. Your mission statement is not set in stone. It will evolve and grow as you do, but it provides a tremendously useful starting point to help you move toward more fulfilling work.

It's often impossible to fit everything we can imagine for ourselves in one mission statement, so it's common to have a couple (or more) in process. I've got several mission statements, depending on which aspect of my work and life I'm focusing on. Here are three of them:

- Through my Five Directions Consulting business, my mission is to help social change organizations increase their effectiveness and "engageability" through mindful awareness.
- My mission is to support love-based social transformation by offering contemplative practices that cultivate compassion and awareness to activists and community organizers.
- My mission is to open up hearts and minds, and to help people to discover more liberating possibilities for their livelihood. I write articles and books, and teach workshops and courses for women in midlife transition who want to cultivate more courage and freedom in their lives.

I hope you find it reassuring to know that if you're a Renaissance-type like me, you don't need to limit yourself to just one! But for the purpose of staying focused on this exercise, it's best to work on one statement at a time.

WHAT DOES A PERSONAL MISSION STATEMENT LOOK LIKE?

Your three-part statement will include each of these components:
1) Your mission
2) The creation, product, or service that you will offer
3) The kind of person/people who will benefit from your creation/product/service, and the need you are addressing

The first part—your mission—will be relevant in every situation. The second two parts are particularly relevant if you want to start your own business or a pilot version of a business (called a Side Hustle, which we'll explore in chapter 11).

To give you an idea of what we're aiming for, let's look more closely at the example of one of my own mission statements:

(1) My mission is to open up hearts and minds, and to help people to discover more liberating possibilities for their livelihood. (2) I write articles and books, and teach workshops and courses (3) for women in midlife transition who want to cultivate more courage and freedom in their lives.

If you look closely, you'll see these three components, which are numbered in the statement:
1. I describe my *why*—my Core Intention, reframed here as my mission.
2. I describe *how* I do it, what it is that I create or provide.
3. I describe *who* this serves and *what need* it meets for them. It's okay to be very specific, in fact, the more specific you can be the better.

As you work through the process that follows, you may find yourself combining two or more steps into the same sentence or writing them in a different order. That's fine. I'm dissecting my mission statement with more precision so you can see each element clearly, but don't worry if yours takes on a different form. What's important is that you have all three elements represented, even if the length or order varies.

HOW TO CREATE YOUR PERSONAL MISSION STATEMENT

I encourage you to take a contemplative approach to the process outlined below. Don't try to do it all in one sitting. Give your mission statement— and yourself—room to breathe. You may want to create a half- or full-day personal retreat and use that as an occasion to center your attention on the questions offered below. (You can find my "Guide to Creating a Personal Retreat" in the Appendix.) I find time in nature can also open you up to new insights. Whenever I'm feeling stuck in my own reflective or creative process, I head outside for a walk with my dog, Lucy, and almost always return home with a new perspective on the blocked place. As you go through this process, I encourage you to take some time outdoors: do some sky gazing for a while, listen to the sounds of the birds in your neighborhood, or even take a short trip somewhere you find beautiful and nourishing to your soul. All of these experiences can deepen the quality of your reflection.

STEP 1

The first part of your mission statement is based on your Core Intention, your "why." If you're not already clear about your Core Intention from the explorations you did back in Key 1, Become Intimate with Your Core Intention, this is the perfect time to revisit that chapter and see what jewels turn up for you.

Here's how my first sentence came out:

My mission is to open up hearts and minds, and to help people to discover more liberating possibilities for their livelihood.

Take a look at your responses to the exercises in Key 1 to help you write this first sentence. In "What Are Your Action Words?," verbs that you rated with a 4 or 5 could make it into this first part of your mission statement. "Open" and "Discover" ranked high for me when I did the exercise.

As you work on this section, dig into the "deeper why" of your mission. For example, say you want to support people to become more comfortable with the dying process. What is the story behind that? Why is that so important to you? How did you come to a place to be able to offer that to the world? Maybe you sat by the bedside of your dying grandmother when you were in your twenties, and that experience touched your heart deeply. It's important for you to be connected with your "why" as you write this part of the mission statement and when you speak with others who are interested in your work. This creates a field of magnetic resonance so that the people you will love to work with can find you, whether they are potential employers or clients.

This part of your mission statement doesn't have to be long. In fact a short and simple phrase is best, as long as it speaks to your heart and soul. While this isn't a scientific analogy, think of what happens when someone goes dowsing for water. When they arrive at a spot where there's underground water, they say the dowsing stick begins to quiver. Something similar should happen to you when you read your mission statement aloud, and particularly this section of it. So … go for the quiver!

STEP 2

This is the most tangible part of your statement, and ideally it should flow naturally from the first part. This is where you ground your Core Intention in an actual form that has the potential to generate income. The big question to answer in this step is: What will you make or what service will you provide?

Here's what my statement looks like with this second component in bold:

(1) My mission is to open up hearts and minds, and to help people to discover more liberating possibilities for their livelihood. **(2) I write articles and books, and teach workshops and courses** *(3) for women in midlife transition who want to cultivate more courage and freedom in their lives.*

There are all kinds of forms that products and services can take. I've collected a number of examples below to illustrate what this second part of the Personal Mission Statement looks like for people who have successfully created a Liberation-Based Livelihood. Each of them has clarified their personal intention, which in turn informs the mission of their business or organization. The products or services they offer flow naturally from that mission. As you read through these examples, can you feel the passion and energy of each person's Core Intention shine through in their mission statement? Perhaps you'll recognize some of your story in one of them, and maybe you'll even find a spark of inspiration for what your livelihood might look like.

LESLIE RINCHEN-WONGMO
Home base: Oxnard, California
Business website: www.threadsofawakening.com

Mission: Leslie Rinchen-Wongmo is a contemporary American textile artist and caretaker of a sacred Tibetan tradition. She stitches bits of silk into elaborate figurative mosaics that bring the transformative images of Buddhist meditation to life. She calls her work "Threads of Awakening" and encourages people to follow the threads of connection and joy in their own lives.

Product/Services: Creates commissioned thangkas (Buddhist textile art), offers an online apprenticeship called Stitching Buddhas to teach others in this tradition.

MARIANNE ELLIOTT

Home base: Wellington, New Zealand

Business website: marianne-elliott.com

Mission: I'm a writer, a yoga teacher, and a human rights consultant. Above all else, I collect, craft, and tell stories. Whether I'm writing a report on violence again toward women in Afghanistan, raising funds for a great cause, helping a client share their good work with the world, or writing my memoir, my craft, my medium, and my passion is story. When people ask me how it's possible to teach yoga online, I tell them I teach yoga through stories. Because stories are how we make sense of the past and how we imagine new futures.

Product/Services: Book: *Zen Under Fire: How I Found Peace in the Midst of War*; online courses, including "30 Days of Courage," "30 Days of Yoga;" in-person workshops and trainings, including Off the Mat, Into the World; writing services for nonprofit organizations, businesses, and individuals.

GENEVIEVE RUSSELL

Home base: Santa Fe, New Mexico

Business website: www.storyportraitmedia.com

Mission: Genevieve's mission is to tell visual stories that inspire us to the core and move the soul to action. She believes that in every community across the nation, there are stories of change. These stories have the power to inspire audiences to act. Genevieve wants to help individuals and organizations deliver their story visually, authentically, and with greatest impact to ensure that it will make a difference. **Product/Services:** Through her business, StoryPortrait Media, Genevieve produces visual storytelling content: photography, documentary film, and socially engaged public art projects, for visionary leaders, organizations, businesses, and artists working toward the empowerment, justice, and well-being of all.

NICHOLA TORBETT

Home base: Oakland, California
Organization website: www.seminaryofthestreet.org
Mission: Nichola believes that powerful transformations are possible when activists actually embody, in community, the alternative values they are fighting for. This is the kind of social change work she wants to catalyze, and this is what inspired Nichola to found Seminary of the Street as a nonprofit organization in 2008.
Services: Seminary of the Street hosts classes and events that support "love warriors working toward the transformation of their communities by embodying God's love in the world." Offerings include "Recovery from the Dominant Culture" 12-step meetings, and a discussion series on "Alternatives to Gentrification."

BRIAN BOGGS

Home base: Asheville, North Carolina
Business website: www.brianboggschairmakers.com
Mission: From the time I was about eight years old I knew I was going to be an artist. I always thought that it would be in the realm of landscape painting and drawing. Then in my early twenties I discovered James Krenov's book on *The Fine Art of Cabinetmaking*. I had never considered that art could take the form of the things we use every day. I could hardly put the book down and found myself reading everything he wrote, one book after the other.

As I was pondering how to begin as a woodworker I discovered a book by John Alexander titled *Make a Chair from a Tree*, a simple approach to the early ways of greenwood chair-making…. Chair-making has provided me with my livelihood, and has excited a stream of creative energy that has filled me with seemingly endless ideas for new chair and tool designs, as well as methods for making them all.

Product/Services: Handmade premium furniture crafted from sustainably sourced lumber. Brian's original designs have grown to encompass outdoor furniture and hospitality installations, all made to order and shipped nationwide. Brian also teaches woodworking all over the world, from Europe to Latin America.

JUNE TANOUE

Home base: Chicago, Illinois

Organization website: www.halauikapono.org

Mission: June Tanoue supports people to live a hula-inspired life of grace, strength, and *aloha*. A native Hawai'ian, June holds a reverence for Hawai'ian cultural beliefs, steeped in respect for the sacredness of nature, and all the many gods and goddesses that inhabit the plants, animals, land, mountains, and ocean. This inspired her to found Halau i Ka Pono, a hula school in Oak Park, Illinois, just outside of Chicago. The organization's mission is to teach the culture and stories of Hawai'i through the joy of its dance: the Hula.

Services: Hula classes for children and adults, private Hula lessons, Zen and Hula retreats, Reiki healing sessions.

FLEQUER VERA

Home base: Cincinnati, Ohio

Business website: www.sustainergy.coop

Mission: Flequer emigrated from Peru, where he grew up working in his family's construction business. Because of his own status as an undocumented worker and his concern for formerly incarcerated people, he became involved in social justice issues. Flequer started Sustainergy in 2013, after learning about alternative business models including Mondragon, a workers' cooperative in Spain. "I saw an opportunity to merge my passions for community organizing, social justice, and community development with my passion for business."[21]

Services: Sustainergy helps homeowners cut energy expenses and improve the comfort of their homes by doing energy audits and insulation.

The co-op model creates well-paying jobs in low-income neighborhoods and gives workers training in sustainable building skills. Sustainergy is a member of the Cincinnati Union Cooperative Initiative.

STEP 3

In this third section, you'll describe the kind of person who is your ideal audience and the need they have that your product/service will meet. This component applies to both jobs and self-employment. If you're job hunting, you can use this section to define the kind of person or organization that you'd like to work for (as well as the cause they serve). This also helps you move into a more empowering mind-set: even if you work for someone else, you have more power over your career destiny than you may think.

Once again, let's use my mission statement as an example, with the third component in bold:

> *(1) My mission is to open up hearts and minds, and to help people to discover more liberating possibilities for their livelihood. (2) I write articles and books, and teach workshops and courses* **(3) for women in midlife transition who want to cultivate more courage and freedom in their lives.**

Many people often skip this step or aren't even aware of it. We get excited about discovering our Core Intention, we figure out what we can make or do with it, but we neglect to discern if there is an actual need for it. Is it something people will be willing to pay money for? (Or some other form of compensation.) This is what Chris Guillebeau, author of *The $100 Startup*, calls the "law of convergence":

> *You must focus continually on how your project can help other people, and why they'll care about what you're offering in the first place. I like to eat pizza, but no matter how passionate I am, it's doubtful I could craft a career around my love for mushrooms and black olives.*[22]

You may be tempted to put things in broad strokes: "This will benefit everyone!" It seems counterintuitive, but the more specific you get in describing your audience, the better your chances of reaching people, including those not necessarily in your target group. Here are a few parameters that can help narrow down your "who":

- Demographics, including gender, ethnicity, age, marital status, number of children. An example: Latino men between forty and sixty years old who are interested in improving their physical well-being.
- Geographic area. You may want to work within your local community, or you may want to set up shop on the Internet so that your reach can extend more globally.
- Who do you most enjoy working with? Who energizes you? What kinds of personality characteristics do they have? Try to describe your people. For example: I love working with self-motivated people who have a great sense of humor.

If you're still searching for your particular service or product, you might want to consider the following four major areas of life in which people tend to need help:

MONEY
- How to get out of debt
- How to create a budget and make it fun to live within it
- How to find scholarships to fund your education

RELATIONSHIPS
- how to be a mindful parent
- how to make dating more fun and less painful
- how to find your soul mate

HEALTH
- how to start a yoga practice
- how to start and stick with a great exercise routine
- how to switch to a gluten-free diet

CREATIVITY/FULFILLMENT/FUN
- how to make a quilt
- how to write a novel
- how to travel around the world on the cheap

Brainstorm what you could create to help meet these needs: workshops, one-to-one training or mentoring, a book, a support group ... what else? Any one of these could become a fun and income-producing Side Hustle. (We'll look at Side Hustles in more detail in chapter 11.)

Another way of finding inspiration is to think about a cause or issue that you are deeply committed to addressing and expressing what you could do. For example,

- I feel close to people who are going through major transitions in their lives and feel passionate about supporting them.
- I love books and believe everyone should have the opportunity to learn to read.
- I am fascinated by yoga and, based on my own experience, I know it has the potential to change lives. I want to share this with others.

This is a good workout for your visioning muscle, the one we spoke about in Key 5, Think Big and Make the Most of Your Resources. A Personal Mission Statement should give you just a bit of a stretch so that you wonder if you can do it … but be grounded in reality enough that it actually is possible.

MISSION STATEMENTS IN REAL LIFE

Your Personal Mission Statement gives you a way to mindfully evaluate work options. Anytime you're considering a potential job or an idea for your own business, match it up against your statement and ask yourself if the elements from your mission are present in it.

Your mission statement can also lead to wonderful work-related serendipity. If you're doing a job search, here's a strategy that can open up new possibilities. Rather than focusing on job titles, look at the mission of the organization or company. You may be better off starting with a job in the mailroom of a place that's aligned with your mission than you would be in a prestigious position in a workplace that has no resonance for you.

Recently I needed to add another income-producing activity to my mix. I came across a job posting from Road Scholar, a nonprofit organization whose mission is to inspire adults to learn, discover, and travel. Here's how they describe their offering: "Our learning adventures open minds to new ideas and deepen understanding of oneself and of the world's peoples, places, cultures, history, and environments."

This was so similar to my Personal Mission Statement that I felt compelled to explore it. I sent in my résumé, was contacted almost immediately for an interview, and was hired as a program guide for

Road Scholar "adventures" in northern New Mexico. I could not have predicted that I'd be leading trips for pay, but it feels just right. My mission statement helped me see that connection.

I've described the process of crafting a Personal Mission Statement in a rather formulaic way, but both time to brew and sudden "a-ha!" moments can help you write a statement that deeply resonates with you. The process I've shared here gives you structure to work within, but listen to your heart and mind as you create yours. Make sure you're not simply imitating someone else—it needs to feel absolutely right to *you*.

Let's close this chapter with a story from Britt Reints, an artist, writer, and author of the book *An Amateur's Guide to the Pursuit of Happiness*. Britt was a reader of my *Liberated Life Project* blog, and tried out a shorter version of the mission statement exercise I shared there. One of the things I appreciate about Britt is her honesty as well as her wicked sense of humor.

> *I had considered learning how to write a mission statement for years. Or at least, I'd come across the idea of a mission statement in numerous self-help books and productivity seminars and thought, "Yeah, that sounds like a good idea, I guess." But mostly I'd left it in the realm of "stuff that sounds good in theory but was probably useless in day-to-day life," like writing down your goals or going through those stupid exercises on the quitting smoking website.*
>
> *Of course, I eventually did start writing down my goals and doing those stupid exercises on the quitting smoking website. And it worked. I suppose that's why I finally decided to give the old mission statement thing a try.*

Britt then describes several tools she used to work on her mission statement, including my "What Are Your Action Words?" exercise (in Key 1), and the Franklin Covey online "Mission Statement Builder" (see the Resources section). Britt continues:

> *I put it aside.*
>
> *That step was huge for me. That step wasn't listed in any of the books, although I had read that figuring out how to write a mission statement could take time. I am generally not great at taking time, at doing nothing, but I'm working on it.*

I came back a few nights later and pulled up the words and sentences that had been cobbled together from the two exercises. I thought about the end of my life, my deathbed, and my inevitable funeral and eulogies. I considered both how I wanted to be remembered and what memories I would likely hold dearest. I began to write.

I put it aside again.

I came back again after a couple more days had passed, and I made some edits. I deleted the superfluous and anything that didn't really resonate with me. I considered my most important roles and ignored anything that I wasn't certain was critical to me at this point in my life.

I was left with this mission statement: My mission is to know and love myself, my neighbor, and my world and to encourage and inspire others to know and love themselves. I am at my best when I am healthy, exploring, learning, inspiring, and connecting. I am proactive about incorporating each of these elements into my life, for I am responsible for being happy, confident, and successful. I find opportunities to use my natural talents of communicating, both listening and sharing. I travel the world and inspire people to identify and embrace what matters most in their lives, and encourage them to reach further. I am guided and identified by the principles of courage, integrity, kindness, and acceptance.

I give my husband and children the courage and faith to live their dreams as well as my unconditional love.

I have faith in destiny and bravely take the path that unfolds before me.

It is not witty or extraordinarily eloquent, and I'm certain it will evolve over the years as I do. It is deeply personal, and I kind of feel like I've just shared with you a video of me doing the ugly cry. Yikes.

I still think the whole thing sounds a little silly, but this mission statement has already served its purpose by being a guide I could consult in confusing times. When we were trying to figure out our next best step—and specifically where we were going to live—I reread these words, and I remembered how important courage was to me and I knew exactly what the most right decision was.[23]

Britt's story emphasizes the intuitive, unfolding nature of this process and illustrates how a mission statement can be essential when making work and life decisions.

CHAPTER 11 Strategies and Tools for Navigating the Three Pathways to Liberation-Based Livelihood

Let's revisit the definition of Liberation-Based Livelihood from chapter 2. First of all, this is a livelihood or career that does not cause harm to yourself or another. Beyond that basic definition, a Liberation-Based Livelihood is one in which you are consciously and consistently connecting your Core Intention to your work, *whatever your work may be.*

It's crucial to recognize that there is no one-size-fits-all Liberation-Based Livelihood. For one person, it may mean launching an inspiring and creative enterprise; for another, it may mean finding a new job or making a conscious choice to reinvest their energy in their current job. First and foremost, this approach to livelihood recognizes and respects our innate differences and needs.

What your Liberation-Based Livelihood looks like will depend on the current circumstances of your life, which includes your responsibilities to others such as family members, economic status, personality, and other factors.

In this chapter, we'll explore three pathways that can lead to your unique manifestation of the Liberation-Based Livelihood:

- Plan Your Exit Strategy
- Love the Job You've Got
- Create Work That You Love

Because this book is meant to serve as a guide throughout different points in your life, you may want to return to this section in the future when you feel a need to reassess your relationship with your work. Life changes such as getting married, moving to a new location, or experiencing a significant change in your financial situation may land you on a different pathway that calls for new strategies.

The starting point for each of these pathways is your Core Intention and your Personal Mission Statement, so make sure to have both in front of you as you read this chapter.

PATHWAY 1: PLAN YOUR EXIT STRATEGY

As you consider how to take your next step toward a Liberation-Based Livelihood, often the first decision you need to consider is can I transform my current job into a vehicle for expressing my Core Intention? Or do I need to let go of it altogether?

This crossroads place is full of potential, and it can go in so many directions—not all of them positive! Bringing mindful awareness into the process greatly increases the possibility that you'll make a healthy decision rather than a reactive one. As I shared in my own story, for many years I tended to leap out of unsatisfactory work situations very quickly. My unhappiness usually followed me into the next job, only to manifest there in new ways.

A good starting point to figure out if it's time to leave your job is to consider if it's harmful to yourself and/or to others. If the answer is "yes," start planning your exit strategy as soon as possible.

What criteria can you use to determine this? Rachel Gillet, careers reporter at *Business Insider*, distilled this insightful list of "16 Signs It's Time to Quit Your Job":

1. You're bored all the time.
2. Your skills aren't being tapped.
3. Your employer's goals and your personal mission don't match up.
4. You've got the boss from hell.
5. You feel like you can't ever win.
6. You're not growing.
7. You always watch what you say.
8. Your company isn't invested in you.
9. You worry about money—all the time.
10. It looks like layoffs are coming.
11. You can't picture yourself at your company in a year.
12. You've got serious trust issues.
13. You're burnt out.
14. You dread Mondays.
15. You can't laugh out loud at work.
16. You just know.

If you find it helpful to draw on more ancient wisdom, traditional Buddhist teachings are quite clear about what does not fall into Right Livelihood. The Vanijja Sutta designates five professions as harmful:

"Business in weapons, business in human beings, business in meat, business in intoxicants, and business in poison" (Vanijja Sutta, AN 5. 177).

You can translate some aspects of this approach to our present times, even if you drop the dogma attached to it. If you're a vegan, then working in a store that sells meat products is going to create a moral dilemma for you. If you have a deep commitment to peace, you probably won't do well working in a factory that produces military arms.

When you find yourself in an occupation that directly contradicts your core values, it's time to leave. There is no adjustment that can resolve that dissonance with your integrity, and the longer you stay, the more of a negative impact this will have on your physical and mental health.

But most cases are not so clear-cut. In today's interconnected and digital economy, it's almost impossible to find a job or industry that even if on its own is benign is not connected to another that is harmful. When I worked in the mental health field, I was in a position to help alleviate some degree of suffering for the patients and clients I came into contact with. At the same time, the prevalent use of psychotropic drugs such as Haldol, which caused terrible side effects, meant I was complicit with a pharmaceutical industry that placed profits above people.

These kinds of moral dilemmas are becoming more common. Is it better to work inside a system that has the potential to do harm—like the mental health system, or the military, or a nuclear lab—and be a helpful presence within it, or is it better to work outside the system and create healthier alternatives? There is no absolute answer to this question. Each of us must create the equation that is most nourishing for us, and our contemplative practice can help us find this.

An extraordinary story of working "inside the belly of the beast" comes from one of the most stressful workplaces I can imagine: the Pentagon. Bart Ives, a civilian who is employed at the Pentagon as an environmental protection specialist, compares it to "walking into a hurricane every day. It's a very high-energy place that makes a lot of demands on individuals, and in this era of downsizing it's even more intense."

Bart also happens to be the president of the Pentagon Meditation Club, originally founded by Ed Winchester in 1976. The group still meets every Friday at noon in the chaplain's conference room. Winchester, who worked as a financial analyst in the Office of the Secretary of Defense, was inspired to start the group by his own practice of Transcendental Meditation. Over the years, he faced resistance of all kinds and was even suspended twice. Winchester said,

I had an experience, an inner experience, of the Pentagon becoming my monastery. I came to the realization that fighting against the system, at least in my mind, wasn't working. Somehow I had to recognize that I was part of the system and the system was a part of me. In the end, I got great satisfaction out of knowing that my little peace might be making a contribution to world peace.[24]

Ed Winchester's story and the legacy he created are remarkable. If you can do something similar, in your own challenging workplace, that's fantastic. But those kinds of environments often wear us down to the point that we're unable to care for ourselves effectively and therefore we are unable to be of service. That was certainly what happened to me at the end of ten years of working in the mental health field. If this describes where you're at, I encourage you to find a way out of your current job situation as soon as possible.

So identifying the level of harm connected to your current job can be a useful and fairly simple way to understand if you need to leave. More often than not, however, the route to finding an answer to this question is more complex and requires further internal detective work.

On the one hand, you may be chomping at the bit to get out of your job for a variety of reasons, including boredom, stress, tensions with your boss, or simply a nagging feeling that you're in the wrong place. If that's the case, try using this question as a litmus test: *With this change, am I moving toward something or running away from something?*

In general, if you're making a change from a place of aversion, it's highly likely that you'll end up in another job with similar results. The big exception is if you're in a situation where working conditions are truly abusive. Remember the basic definition of Right Livelihood: make sure you are not in a work environment that is harming you.

Lyndon related the process he went through in leaving an unfulfilling position as a marketing professional before he found his Liberation-Based Livelihood as a chaplain:

Initially I wanted to leave my job right away because I had a difficult relationship with the supervisor, in addition to the stress of the job. Back then I did loving kindness practice every day (note: you can find this practice in the Resources section). When I got to the part where you direct the practice to a person you struggle with, there was no question who I was going to think about! That supervisor. Integrating mindfulness practice with that job

*changed how I was in relationship to that person. I was able to
leave on good terms.*

*I didn't leave that job feeling like I was running away from
something as much as I felt I was going to something. I don't
think I'd have been able to make that shift without loving
kindness practice. It wasn't quick—I did about a year of that.
But when I did leave, I didn't feel like I was giving up. And
I certainly didn't leave with a bad relationship. I was able to
improve the situation.*

Like Lyndon, you can ask yourself what lessons you still need to learn
before you let the job go. What unfinished business is there for you?
You can also draw on some of the strategies in Pathway 2 (Love the Job
You've Got). When you work through the process in a mindful way, you
create a situation where you can leave with integrity and start your new
adventure with a clean slate.

The other possible scenario is that you may realize you are seriously
unhappy and you need to quit but you just can't do it. Let's take a look at
three of the most common sources of resistance that keep us stuck and
see how we can deflate them of their power.

1. I Need the Security That My Current Job Offers Me.

As we explored in Key 4, the idea of "security" can trap and deaden us,
and it may keep us clinging to jobs that no longer serve us. We avoid
taking action because we're afraid of the risk involved. However, there
is a creative way to reframe "risk." One of my favorite writers on this
matter is Chris Guillebeau, author of *The $100 Startup*. Here's how
Chris puts it:

*Entrepreneurship has traditionally been viewed as risky because
it involves investment and uncertainty. But these days, you can
start a business in a short amount of time, using the skills you
already have and without spending a lot of money. Even if success
takes a few iterations to achieve, there is very little downside.*

*Contrast this reality with the reality of today's job market. Real
unemployment among young people, even college graduates, is often
fifteen percent or more. Many people are underemployed by working at Starbucks or taking other low-level jobs because they can't
find work in the field for which they trained. Layoffs are rampant,
and most "real jobs" allow for little flexibility or real advancement.*
Which is the safer choice?[25]

It's also important to realize that there are ways to mitigate risk. If you discern that you're ready to leave your job and you want to pursue Pathway 3 (Create Work That You Love), you can do a Side Hustle first—slowly dipping your toe into waters of self-employment while continuing to hang on to your job. You can also become more intentional about putting things in place now (like a healthier savings account and developing your skills for your new work) that will enable you to make the leap when the time is right. This doesn't have to be an all-or-nothing proposition.

When we focus on your Action Plan in chapter 12, we'll look more closely at smart ways you can prepare yourself now to make a big shift down the road.

2. I Don't Know If I Have the Energy to Look for a New Job or Start My Own Business.

That's a good question and only you can really answer it. A job search does take a lot of time and energy, but you can also enter into it like it's an adventure. I often call my job search a "treasure hunt." (Hmm, I'm noticing a theme here, along with the "Mining for Gold" exercise!) I get out my journal and sketch a map of all the possible places where I might find that treasure, from businesses and organizations that are doing work I really admire to former supervisors who are big fans of my work and may have connections to a great job or project. When I cultivate that spirit of openness and curiosity, I have much more energy to go through an extended job search, and it's a lot more fun!

If you're considering starting your own business, it's true that you need the gumption and persistence to stick with it. To succeed, you need to learn how to capitalize on your setbacks rather than let them overwhelm you. There is an entrepreneurial attitude that you either need to have or be willing to develop. Without that, starting your own business will be a huge struggle.

So yes, it's important to be honest with yourself and recognize your limitations. But also notice where you may be underestimating yourself and your capacity to grow and practice new skills. Remember you don't have to do everything yourself—you can delegate or outsource tasks that don't fall in your strength zone (a lesson from Key 6, Build a Circle of Allies and Ask for Help).

3. I Don't Love My Job, but I Don't Hate It.

The "I don't love my job, but I don't hate it either" syndrome is one where your thoughts often run along a groove like this: "I don't love my job, but I don't hate it. The salary is okay and the benefits are good. To be honest, I'm not sure I know what I really want to do for work. I'm afraid if I leave my job now, I'll regret it later."

This might be the toughest one of all. We can spend months, years, even decades in this place. Sailors call it the "doldrums," a low-pressure zone around the equator where the prevailing winds are ultra calm and sailboats get trapped for days and weeks.

Let's start with this assumption: if you're really fine with where you're at, there's no need to change anything. I'm guessing if you're reading this book, though, you have a nagging feeling that's not enough. At some point it's going to be crucial for you to honor that intuition. By continuing to ignore it, you run the risk of apathy, depression, and even anger.

I find it helpful to think about my "expiration date" in any given endeavor, whether that's a project, a job, or something else. Like milk that has gone beyond its expiration date, we go sour. That's not good for anybody. I can usually feel when I'm arriving at the expiration date because I start to get irritated and impatient with others (and myself). Sometimes it's good to push through those periods of time and learn something about ourselves. But at a certain point, we've learned all there is to learn.

It's important to notice and honor this impulse to make a change. It may not need to happen right away, but you can start planning for how to make the change in the best possible way.

QUESTIONS FOR REFLECTION

Here are some questions to ask yourself to help you evaluate if it's time to make your exit:

- Is my job harmful to me and/or to others? Is it harmful to the planet?
- In leaving this job, would I be moving toward something or running away from something? What unfinished business do I have that might carry over into a new work situation?
- What is the risk involved in leaving my job? Am I ready and willing to take that risk? And what is the potential payoff?
- How close am I to my "expiration date" on my current job? Will I turn into sour milk soon if I stay?

PATHWAY 2: LOVE THE JOB YOU'VE GOT

You may discover that you don't need or want to leave your present job; you just need to find a way to fall in love with it again (or for the first time). There may be very good reasons for staying where you are for a while, even if it's not perfect. Maybe you have a family to support and a reliable income source is necessary. Sometimes you gotta do what you gotta do to pay rent and keep food on the table, right? And there can be other legitimate reasons why you're not ready or able to take on the risks that come with Pathways 1 and 3.

In this section, we'll look at three ways to learn how to love the job you've got, or at least to neutralize the more negative feelings you may have about it. These strategies can also apply to a job you start after leaving a toxic work environment (see Pathway 1). If it's not yet your dream job, you can make some adjustments so that you're in a good relationship to it as you build other possibilities (see Pathway 3).

1. CONNECT YOUR CORE INTENTION TO YOUR WORK

I once heard a yoga teacher use a wonderful saying to describe how a minor adjustment in posture can make a major impact: "The difference between heaven and hell is half an inch." You can apply this principle to your current work situation. It may only take a slight shift in perspective to have a completely different relationship to your work, and one of the most effective ways to do this is to bring more awareness of your Core Intention to your job.

When you connect your Core Intention (and by extension your Personal Mission Statement) to your job, you'll often find deeper purpose and meaning than what might be apparent on the surface. For example, after going through the exercises in this book, you've clarified that you are here on the planet to offer healing. Yet you work the cash register at the local Piggly Wiggly grocery store, which seems completely unrelated to being a healer. Even so, you can make a conscious choice to meet every person you encounter in the store with compassion and kindness. By doing so, you are bringing that healing quality to your work, and you've turned it into a Liberation-Based Livelihood.

Martha used this strategy to "fall in love" with her longtime job as a hairdresser. When she completed her Mining for Gold exploration from Key 1, she noticed a few words kept showing up across her history of jobs, projects, and volunteer placements: *collaboration, support, connection, social, fun, creative.* The one word that turned up in everything she had done was *service.* Martha recalled,

> *This was such an obvious discovery for me but I just saw it in a whole new way. There are so many great things about having a job that makes people happy and I have deep connections with*

many of my clients. I get to witness their lives, and listen to their stories. I realized that I love what I do!

This insight gave Martha renewed energy to reengage with her career. This is the Personal Mission Statement she wrote for herself and refers to frequently before going to work:

My mission is to be open and loving, to encourage creative connection. I will support my clients to help them feel better about themselves. I will do this by providing the best hair services I am capable of and offering them my full attention, as a witness to their lives.

2. DO YOUR INNER WORK AND REMEMBER THE 6 KEYS

When I started my *Liberated Life Project* blog in 2010, I chose the tagline "Freedom is an inside job" as a quick way to convey my philosophy: No matter what the external circumstances of our life, we can work with our mind to find liberation from suffering, and to create a more just and beautiful world for ourselves and everyone.

Some of the most profound examples of "liberated lives" come, in fact, from people who have been incarcerated. Take Nelson Mandela, who was imprisoned for twenty-seven years following arrest for his involvement with an anti-apartheid militant resistance group in South Africa. During that time, his friend Desmond Tutu said, "Nelson Mandela evolved from an angry young man into someone who grew in magnanimity and in his understanding of the point of view of the other." Mandela was able to break out of the prison of his own anger to step into a much greater version of himself. In the process, he helped to dissolve apartheid and create a new South Africa.

While Nelson Mandela was an extraordinary human being, even us mere mortals can do some major alchemy when we apply this principle to our lives and work. Susan, a graduate of Fall in Love with Your Work, worked as a fundraising professional with a nonprofit organization. Her job was to solicit donations or gifts and "close" them, bringing in much-needed infusions of cash to her organization. She shared this story:

I wasn't happy with my work and was ready to leave my job. I had come to that conclusion because of some leadership choices at my workplace and also because I thought the job wasn't in alignment with my deeper values. But I loved the organization and its mission, so I thought I'd give it one last shot. That's why I signed up for Fall in Love with Your Work.

The exercises about valuing ourselves (in Key 2) really made an impact on me. Throughout my life I have often felt that what I did wasn't that important. I was having a hard time with one exercise and then you suggested that I journal on three things that I value about myself. I found that so helpful and still do that practice each day. Some of the things I've learned to notice and value: my commitment to practice even in the midst of difficulty, my commitment to make the world a better place, my integrity. Once I experienced how to value myself more authentically, that created a big internal shift.

Then things happened externally that also made a big difference. My boss, whom I found extremely difficult, left the organization. As soon as she left I knew that the energy was going to shift, and that it would be okay. After that, I closed a couple of very large gifts to the organization. That came after a nearly two-year drought during which I'd had difficulty closing big gifts.

I felt like the winds shifted. I can't say it was all a result of the work I did, but I think I created the conditions internally where I could go with it. It was like putting my sails up so I could catch the winds when they shifted.

Now I feel so lucky to have the job I have. It's an amazing organization, a community based on love and respect. I am so happy to be part of it, and so happy that I didn't give it up.

Here are a few ways to focus on your inner work and transform your relationship with your job:

Apply the 6 Keys

Take note of your complaints about your job, because that's where you'll get the best clues about your growing edges. Then consider which of the Keys you can strengthen as a way to meet that challenge.

- If you're unhappy about how much work your boss assigns to you, the opportunity is to value yourself enough to raise this issue with them and propose creative solutions. It might also be a signal that you need to practice setting boundaries so you take better care of yourself. All of this is within the domain of Key 2 (Value Your Gifts and Your Time).

- If you're bored and restless at your job, what innovative project can you dream up that gives you a chance to express your Core Intention? Dream big. This is the lesson from Key 5 (Think Big and Make the Most of Your Resources).
- If you feel isolated at your workplace, the invitation is to remember you don't have to be a lone wolf. Who can you reach out to, either within your office or in your wider circle of friends and mentors? Key 6 reminds us that the people in our lives are our greatest resource (Build a Circle of Allies and Ask for Help).

Turn Up the Volume on What's Good

It can be easy to focus on what's going wrong. Take an inventory and ask yourself what's going well in your current situation and how you can capitalize on that. Here are a few places to start looking:

- Is there a coworker with whom you've got shared interests and you'd like to collaborate? How can you make that happen?
- Does your workplace offer ongoing training or continuing education opportunities? How can you take advantage of that?
- Is your supervisor someone you respect who is willing to mentor you so that you can move closer toward some of your professional goals?

By turning our attention to what's working instead of what's lacking, we can make a big shift in our level of job satisfaction.

Bring Your Contemplative Practice into Your Workplace

If you have established a regular contemplative practice, you've got a powerful game changer in your tool kit. You can apply your practice to any frustrating situation in your workplace.

In *Real Happiness at Work*, meditation teacher Sharon Salzberg describes the "3 Pillars of Happiness in the Workplace" that come about through practice:

- **Balance**: differentiating between who you are and what your job is
- **Concentration**: focusing without being swayed by distraction
- **Compassion**: being aware of and sympathetic to the humanity of ourselves and others
- **Resilence**: recovering from defeat, frustration, or failure

- **Communication and Connection**: understanding that everything we do and say can further connection or take away from it
- **Integrity**: bringing your deepest ethical values to the workplace
- **Meaning**: infusing the work you do with relevance for your own personal goals
- **Open Awareness**: seeing the big picture and not being held back by self-imposed limitations

Remember the Tree of Contemplative Practices from chapter 3? Your practice can be anything from sitting meditation to gardening to yoga (and more). Your practice helps you to cultivate the qualities that Sharon names above and this, in turn, can increase your equanimity and even joy in your current job.

Susan, the nonprofit professional you met earlier, was able to shift her attitude about her job by working through the practices in Key 2, and learning how to value herself. In addition, her longtime meditation practice helped her to develop the resilience she needed to get through that rough period in her job, as well as the openness to see it (and herself) in a new light.

Over the course of working with the 6 Keys, you may have noticed some of your own patterns. Perhaps you've seen that you are easily frustrated when obstacles arise, or that you have a tendency to get bored and distracted, or that you often feel fearful in response to something new. While you may feel discouraged by this, this awareness is actually a gift! In the moment when you are able to stop and finally see that pattern, you have created a choice point rather than an unconscious action.

Here's a practice: tune into the pattern that has become clearer to you as you practice. Then, ask yourself: "What is the quality that I would like to cultivate as a way to transform that pattern?" For example, if you have noticed a tendency to become frustrated and give up when something becomes challenging, you may want to develop persistence.

Give yourself time to do some journaling on both the pattern as well as the quality you are developing in response to it. Please remember that this is not about punishment or forcing a change; it is about trusting the power of gentle noticing to bring about transformation.

The heart of "practice" is so much about being able to take a step back and, in that step, being able to change your perspective. There are some very tangible reminders in everyday life that can serve as "mindfulness bells" to help bring you back to that spacious place of practice and support the gentle transformation of those patterns. These little gifts from the universe take the form of sights, sounds, smells, and other kinds of experiences. In our "ordinary" reality, we might take them for granted and let them slip by, and even get caught up in anxiety or fear around them. However, if you can look at them from a new vantage point, they become allies in this process of waking up. Here are some of them:

- the ringing of your phone
- the song of a bird
- a stop sign as you drive to work
- a stone that you keep in your pocket
- a flower in a vase on your desk
- the first email or text that turns up on your device in the morning

How can you create a "living mindfulness bell" for your practice off the cushion? You might want to choose one of the "events" from the list above, or you may be inspired to designate some other stimulus that frequently pops up in your life as your mindfulness bell.

We are invited in these everyday ways to reawaken, as if from a trance, to the present moment. That might mean you take an opportunity to breathe deeply once or twice, to clear your mind of whatever might be going on in that moment, and reset yourself for a new experience of reality. We are invited in these everyday ways to reawaken, as if from a trance, to the fresh moment here, just now.

For example, if you choose the ringing of your phone, you can experiment with this: every time your phone rings, wait for three rings before you answer it. (This is a practice I learned years ago when I was an intern at Parallax Press!) In the period of time that you are waiting, reconnect with your body and your breath and allow your mind to settle. Then see how that changes your experience of answering the phone and connecting with the person on the other end.

3. SHIFT THE EXTERNAL FACTORS

In the classic book *The 7 Habits of Highly Successful People*, Stephen Covey describes a simple model to consider challenges and problems we encounter. Within the "Circle of Concern" are situations that we care about but aren't in a position to impact (at least on first glance). Within the "Circle of Influence" are situations where we actually do have the power to change the outcome.

Here are a couple of work-related examples:

Circle of Concern: "Our company's main product is a violent video game that I would never let my own kids play. I feel morally conflicted about receiving money from these profits." Unless you have a seat on the board of directors of your company, you are probably not in a position to impact their choice of products.

Circle of Influence: "I feel stressed out from picking up the slack for my coworker who's not doing his job." In this scenario, you have the ability to break your codependent tendency to make up for a coworker's bad habits. That may not be easy to do, but you can make choices that will influence the outcome, which in this case is your stress level.

Covey's main point is that successful people are proactive and spend the majority of their energy in the Circle of Influence. If you feel burned out, consider this model and notice where you may be spending too much time and energy on matters that fall into your Circle of Concern, and not enough on those that fall into your Circle of Influence.

As you identify matters that fall into the Circle of Influence, here are a few strategies that can improve your situation. The first step is to identify the conditions that would support you to thrive at your job.

Negotiate Working Conditions That Support What's Important to You

This is easiest to do if you have a long relationship with your employer and they know how invaluable you are. It's still possible to do this even if you are fairly new in your position.

- Work from home one day a week. If you need to convince your supervisor, you can refer them to numerous studies like one from the Stanford Graduate School of Business that indicate that telecommuters are more productive (and happier) than their office counterparts. (Check out "How to Make a Case for Telecommuting" in the Resources section.)
- Have flexible hours. Start your workday at 10:30 rather than 9 a.m. so you don't have to deal with frustrating rush hour traffic.
- Take on a new and more creative responsibility.
- Let go of a current task that is draining your energy ... invite your supervisor to help you brainstorm how this task could be handled more efficiently.

- Create a new project at work that links up with your passions.
- Next, schedule a time to speak with your supervisor and bring your request(s) forward. Let them know that you are very enthusiastic about bringing your best self to the workplace, and that finding solutions to these requests will help to make that possible. The kind of response you get will give you a good deal of information about how viable it is for you to continue in your current job.

Like Susan, Beth is also a nonprofit fundraising professional who participated in Fall in Love with Your Work. She shared this story about making a request for a change in her working conditions:

I felt restless and unsure about my job as a Regional Gift Advisor for Best Friends Animal Society. I was feeling happy (with the cause) but not satisfied. I knew I had skills and gifts that were not being utilized, and I missed using them. As I began to hone in on what was missing from my work, I also investigated possibilities of making a change. My first choice was to remain with the organization, because I feel passionate about the mission and vision.

I researched tasks and titles at other companies that seemed related to what I wanted to do—make people happy and connect them with their purpose. I looked into Chief Happiness Officer job descriptions as well as Donor Recognition duties and ideas. My work for the past twenty years has been in fundraising, which includes some donor recognition duties, but I really wanted to focus more on them.

Then I created a proposal that outlined both of these jobs, and ran it by a few people who were supportive and agreed that there was a need at my organization. With their feedback, I edited the presentation and shared it with senior management. While they did not wish to let me stop fundraising, they saw the value in both ideas. Given our organization's budget and current structure, the one that made the most sense was the Donor Recognition job. I was supported to cut my fundraising portfolio and responsibilities in half while becoming the Manager of Donor Recognition and Experience. My hope is to excel at the latter to the point where I may phase out my fundraising duties and focus full-time on making donors feel good about supporting our organization.

Now I am both happy and satisfied with my work, because I'm using a fuller complement of my skills and passions. I am helping my teammates create special experiences and personalized reports to show the organization's top supporters how grateful we are.

Ask for a Raise

Money is not everything, but it can be a significant factor in workplace satisfaction. If you've been with your company or organization for more than two years and you've been doing a good job and have not yet received a raise, then your contributions are not being recognized and affirmed. Over time, that can erode your job satisfaction as well as your own sense of value. Remember Key 2, Value Your Gifts and Time? This is a time to exercise your self-valuing muscle and make a case for why you've earned a raise.

Twice in my professional career I've requested more compensation. Each time, I had to face my own issues with how I valued my work, as well as codependent tendencies to think that perhaps I was asking too much of my employer. This is common especially with women. As I noted in Key 5 (Think Big and Make the Most of Your Resources), internalized oppression can turn up in many places and asking for a raise is a big one. Perhaps the most important thing you can do to prepare for making this request is to reconnect with your Core Intention and review the "Recognizing Your Worth" practice from Key 2. You are, in a very real sense, irreplaceable, and if you go into this conversation anchored in that place, you will convey your value in a strong way.

A few more tips on how to ask for a raise:

- Be prepared. Research salaries in your field so you have credible information about the going rate for comparable positions. Check out the website www.payscale.com to get an idea of what you're worth.
- Collect testimonials from customers or clients who have been thrilled with your work.
- Set up a time to make the request to your supervisor in person—don't rely on email for this important conversation. If you have an annual job review, that's a good time to make a case for a salary increase.

Not every company or organization is in a position to increase salaries, no matter how great a job you've done and how much they appreciate you. If this is the case in your workplace, you still have leverage to request other changes that would increase your satisfaction with your job. Maybe a flex-time schedule would help you, or new and more interesting work assignments, or more vacation time. Make a list ahead of time and be prepared to ask for what you need if higher financial compensation is not an option.

Become an Agent of Change in Your Workplace

You may feel passionately about addressing low wages or substandard working conditions, or perhaps the company you work for makes a product that goes against your values. Speak with others in your workplace who have similar concerns and talk about how you can develop a collective voice to address them with management.

Perhaps one of the most famous examples of a workplace rabble-rouser is Crystal Lee Sutton, the real-life union organizer who was the inspiration for the 1979 film *Norma Rae*. In 1973, Sutton was working in a North Carolina textile factory, where she earned $2.65 an hour. For the mother of three children, this was not a living wage. Sutton took a leadership role in trying to unionize other workers at the plant in order to increase pay and improve poor working conditions. She was fired for doing so, leading to the climactic moment portrayed in the movie: Sutton wrote the word "Union" on a piece of cardboard and stood up on a table as the police (who had been summoned by the management) came to remove her from the factory. As she slowly turned around on the table to show the sign to her coworkers, they turned off their machines in solidarity with her until the whole factory resounded in powerful silence. In the next year, the Amalgamated Clothing and Textile Workers Union won the right to represent three thousand employees at seven plants, including the one that Sutton had worked in.

Workplace activism is getting a digital upgrade with the arrival of the website coworker.org, which enables employees to connect virtually, identify issues they want to address together, and aggregate data to help them build their case. A recent campaign organized on the site by more than eleven thousand Wells Fargo workers resulted in the bank ending its controversial practice of high-pressured sales goals.

This can be a risky path and it's not for everyone. But for you it may be the right one ... perhaps this is the time to channel your inner Norma Rae!

QUESTIONS FOR REFLECTION

Here are some questions to ask yourself about your relationship to the job you've got and how it might get better for you:

- Where is there more potential to express my Core Intention in my current job?
- How can I use my Personal Mission Statement as a source of inspiration for my current job?
- Which of the 6 Keys is least developed in my life? How might I strengthen it to find more meaning and satisfaction in my current job?
- Where am I spending most of my time and energy: in the Circle of Concern or the Circle of Influence?
- What conditions would I like to change that will make a significant difference in how I feel about my current job? What strategies would I like to try out for this purpose?

PATHWAY 3: CREATE WORK THAT YOU LOVE

If clarity has hit you like a thunderbolt and you realize you're tired of trying to fit into other peoples' boxes and you're ready to create something new, what do you do next?

Perhaps you can relate to this story from Laura, another Fall in Love with Your Work graduate:

> *I applied for an administrative position with our local community college more than four months ago. The process to apply for any position there, as with many companies, involves setting up an account, registering, and then completing their online application. They don't want a résumé or cover letter. The entire application process is automated for the employer. Yesterday I received a "Thanks but no thanks letter"—four months later. Which is better than most companies that send nothing. Ever.*
>
> *Job hunting has changed significantly with technology but this isn't a rant about technology. This is more of a musing out loud about being frustrated and facing an uncertain future.*
>
> *When all efforts yield the same results, expecting something different is the definition of insanity. And I've had enough of living in crazy town. Perhaps it's a clear sign that the old way of thinking, "I need someone to give me a job/someone has to hire me," needs an upgrade.*
>
> *Instead of trying to fit my experience, skills, and value into some boxes in an online application, what if I were to create my own new reality? It can't be any crazier than what I'm doing right now.*

I love Laura's story. The way she embraces the idea of creating her own reality reminds me a lot of the feeling I had when I left my mental health career and dove right into graduate study of cultural anthropology. It really did take a certain amount of crazy intuitive wisdom to make that leap, and I am forever grateful that I did.

We tend to think in the templates given to us; so when it comes to getting a fresh start with our work, that usually means one of two things: 1) get a new job, or 2) start a small business. If you don't feel ready to do either of these, you may give up entirely.

There are plenty of great books and courses on how to find a job or start a business; I've included a number of my favorites in the Resources section. Rather than reinvent the wheel, I want to introduce you to a different way of thinking about this Pathway so you can reduce that feeling of overwhelm and start creating work you love.

EXPANDING YOUR POSSIBILITIES

First, take another look at your Personal Mission Statement. For a moment, set aside the expectation that you need to have a full-time job to fulfill your mission, that you have to get a position with a specific title (e.g., "I am a psychotherapist," or "I am a schoolteacher"), or that you have to be wild and crazy enough to start your own business (though maybe you are).

What if the whole point is to spend more of your time doing what you love and expressing your Core Intention? But this doesn't necessarily have to come through a job. In the same way that we unhooked the concepts of "money" and "value" back in Key 2, let's unhook "job" and "work."

The following list offers a multitude of options to consider beyond a conventional full-time job. Some are "paid" in the traditional sense that you can receive money for doing them. For other options, the compensation comes in the form of room and board rather than a salary, or you receive training and mentorship. Even if not all of them are realistic for you, allow this list to begin to expand your sense of possibilities. (See the Resources section for specific ways to follow up on many of these ideas.)

17 ALTERNATIVE WAYS TO MAKE A LIVING

1) International and domestic service opportunities, like the Peace Corps and AmeriCorps.

2) Become a resident at a spiritual center. These centers look for people who understand that work can be a spiritual practice and often offer support in the form of room and board, and sometimes a stipend.

3) Become an intern to learn a specific skill. Note that internships are for people of all ages, not just young folks!

4) Become a consultant—offer your expertise to companies or organizations.

5) Teach a group of people a subject that you know well and that they would like to learn. This could be anything from changing the oil in your car to executive leadership skills.

6) Create a Side Hustle—a small version of your own business that you can do while holding on to your current job. More on this below.

7) Start your own business or nonprofit organization.

8) Imagine your dream project (e.g., writing a book, making a film, opening a show of your art at a local gallery). Then invite support from friends or use a crowdfunding platform like Indiegogo or Patreon to make it happen.

9) Apply for a fellowship to be supported to do what you love.

10) If you're an artist, begin selling your work on a site like Etsy.

11) If you're a writer, self-publish your book and sell it.

12) If you're a photographer, sell your photos to a site like Fotolia.

13) If you're a musician, head to your local town center, become a street performer, and pass a hat.

14) Join a time bank in your hometown, or organize one if it doesn't exist. Exchange your time and talents with others in your community, and help create a "gift economy."

15) If you love to travel and have dreamed about living abroad, get trained to teach English to students in another country. And no, you don't necessarily need to know the language of the country to which you're moving.

16) If you love to travel and love being in nature, become a campground host for a season or longer. These are mostly volunteer jobs, but sometimes there is a stipend.

17) Become a house sitter as a way to travel the world for very little money, or as a way to live in your local area on a tight budget. The time you free up from working at a conventional job can then be spent doing more of what you love.

WORK MODES

Let's break this down even more. The work landscape has changed dramatically in the past decade; a 2015 report from the US Government Accountability Office concluded that more than forty percent of all workers now have "contingent" or nonconventional jobs.[26] This list identifies some of the forms that work now takes:

- **Employee** You work for someone else for regular wage and benefits. You (generally) show up at their location and hours. You may be working in a small, medium, or large company.
- **Nonprofit professional** You start a nonprofit organization or work for one as freelancer, contractor, or employee.
- **Contractor** You work for yourself, often for a primary client or project. This is usually close to full-time with a set project start and end date. You work at your own location and hours.
- **Freelancer** You work for yourself on a variety of projects for a variety of clients. The size and scope of clients often fluctuates.
- **Small business owner** You own a business where you develop and sell products and/or services to a specific market. Your business may be primarily online or brick and mortar, or a combination of both.
- **Social entrepreneur** You own a for-profit business with an agenda to solve a social or environmental problem. Some or all of the profits may be used to support a cause. Examples include Toms Shoes and Ben & Jerry's ice cream.
- **Independent producer** You're a creator of some kind (writer, artist, musician, filmmaker, etc.) and you raise funds through crowdsourcing (such as Indiegogo or Patreon); you sell your creations on sites such as Etsy; you may have patrons or corporate sponsors.
- **Collaboration** In the new world of work, individuals might team up with other freelancers and entrepreneurs to work on group projects in addition to their own work. With this team, you create and offer products or services that none of you could do alone.

[Thanks to Pamela Slim for including a foundational version of this list in her book, *Body of Work: Finding the Thread That Ties Your Story Together*.]

Each of these work modes has a unique flavor and some will fit better with your life and temperament than others. For example, if you have a high need for the security of a regular paycheck and benefits, "employee" is probably a better match for you than "freelancer." "Contractor" falls somewhere in the middle, as it can provide reliable income, usually from the same client or group of clients, but gives you more flexibility than you would have as an employee.

You don't need to be limited to just one of the above. While eighty percent of your work might come in the "employee" mode, you can venture into the "freelancer" or "independent producer" mode with the remaining twenty percent of your time. Or any other combination that works. You can also change the equation as time goes on, in order to better serve your needs.

Jami's story is an excellent example of how to stay fluid with the forms your work takes:

> *About half of my career as a musician, I also worked part-time as a nurse. I was lucky enough to have nursing as a skill because the hourly wage was good and it was really flexible. After my album* Hidden Sky *was released, I let go of nursing completely. Sometimes I think of going back to it, but more as a way to stay home instead of all the touring that goes with being a musician. And I miss that physical one-to-one connection with people. Sometimes I think about that as a next step, or starting a nonprofit that would weave it all together. At this point in my life, I don't see it as a failure if I have to get a job to support my music. At one point I did. Now I just feel like it's not a big deal for me to roll up my sleeves and get a job. In fact sometimes I feel like it would be a relief.*

If you need to change something and you're not quite ready to find a new job or start a business, consider how you might add another work mode into your mix. Here are some possibilities:

- Can you teach yoga at your local community center? [freelancer or volunteer]
- Can you volunteer at a local nonprofit whose mission you really love, as a way to get your foot in the door? [nonprofit]

- Can you experiment with putting some of your artwork for sale on Etsy? [independent producer]
- Can you think of other people whose work you admire that you can team up with to create something? For example, you're a filmmaker and you know someone who is great at gathering stories and writing. The two of you could collect oral histories from neighborhood elders and create a book, and set up an Indiegogo campaign to fund the project. [collaboration + independent producer]

FINDING THE RIGHT DANCE STEP

My own meandering path toward a Liberation-Based Livelihood is probably not one that any career counselor would recommend. It has veered off in unplanned and unexpected directions and at times has felt chaotic. Yet looking back on it with more perspective, it's now clear to me how all the pieces fit together to bring me to a place where I truly love what I do for a living. Even the chaotic or dissonant-seeming sections served to move me toward some resolution down the road. More than anything my career seems like a grand dance. There has been a flow, and even when it seemed like nothing was happening, there was still movement. At different points in time particular dance steps were called for, and some steps have been repeated throughout the dance.

As I reflected on this career "dance," here are the steps I identified:

- **Glide** Periods of time when you are at the same job or in the same field for a number of years.
- **Pivot** Shifting positions within the same professional field in order to realign yourself more closely with your Core Intention, or making adjustments to other important factors in your workplace (e.g., going from full-time to flex hours so you can stay home more with family).
- **Side Hustle** Innovative ways to make money alongside your regular job. This step allows you to maintain a reliable stream of income while opening new doors.
- **Big Leap** Making a big change from one career to another (like my leap from mental health to anthropology), or from one modality to a dramatically different one (like going from a full-time job to living on an ashram). Big Leaps can be voluntary or involuntary (as in when we are laid off from a job).

When I reviewed my career dance card, here's what I noticed. In the early part of my career, all of my work was in "employee" mode because that was the form most familiar to me. In recent years, I've increased my comfort level with work forms that have a higher level of risk involved (e.g., small business owner, independent producer). This has helped to keep my own career dance vibrant and connected to my Core Intention. A combination of factors contributed to my becoming more at ease with risk: in some cases, like my unexpected job loss during the 2008 economic crash, I had limited choices, and this pushed me toward small business ownership; during periods of time that I had built up a healthy Freedom Fund, I could afford to take more risks; and finally, the more you do it, the easier it gets! Over the past decade, I've gotten much better at taking dance steps that flow from my heart and my Core Intention, and that's made all the difference in how much I love my work.

Let's take a closer look at each dance step, when you might choose it, and how to make the most of each one:

Glide

There's nothing wrong with periods of stability when you're in the same job or are working in the same company or organization for a number of years. But you need to use that time in a conscious way, otherwise it's all too easy to slip into a trance of "I'm fine just where I'm at," when your spirit is calling you in a new career direction. The Glide can be a wonderful time to gather all types of resources so that you're in a better position to make a Big Leap when the moment is right.

When you're in a Glide, you can set an intention to develop technical skills, such as learning a new software program, or people skills, such as improving your management techniques. The skills that I developed during my long Glide stretches later became the foundation for new career directions. Even though I eventually left the mental health profession, the ten years I spent working in that field were not in vain. During that time I cultivated skills in counseling and facilitating that I now draw on as a coach and teacher. When you move through a Glide period with intentionality, nothing will be wasted. You might be pleasantly surprised by how your skills and resources adapt to help you meet changing conditions in a new job or work mode.

You can also use this time to grow your "Freedom Fund," a savings account that gives you a cushion to make choices about your next professional move from positivity rather than fear. As a general rule, a

Freedom Fund should provide you with enough to cover at least three months of your essential expenses (including rent or mortgage, utilities, groceries, healthcare, transportation). If you have no money to fall back on, you may justify your own fears about not taking your next step toward a Liberation-Based Livelihood because it's too risky.

If you're in a Glide, consider what it is that you would like to move toward, using your Personal Mission Statement as a guide. Then, during this time of professional stability, ask yourself:

- Are there specific skills I can develop or improve during this period?
- Are there relationships I may want to deepen with people who may eventually assist me to make a Big Leap?
- Is this a time when I can start or grow my Freedom Fund?

Pivot

If some aspects of your professional field or in your workplace are nourishing but you notice yourself reaching that "expiration date" I talked about in Pathway 2, an alternative to making a Big Leap is to do a Pivot.

One of my own Pivots came after three years of serving as the executive director for the Buddhist Peace Fellowship, a nonprofit organization in the San Francisco Bay Area. I was exhausted from the stress of fundraising and staff management and realized I needed to make a change, but I still loved the organization's mission, to serve as a catalyst for socially engaged Buddhism. Another position opened up as editor of the organization's quarterly journal; it was much better suited to my temperament and skill set. I let the board of directors know I wanted to step down from the executive director job and move into the editor position. It was an unconventional move—in a sense I demoted myself and I took a pay cut—but I was much happier in the new role and felt a huge sense of relief. I also got to continue being at a place that was doing work I truly believed in.

If you sense that you need to make a change but not necessarily a Big Leap, here are a few things to consider:

- Is there another position at your company or organization that will better allow you to express your Core Intention?
- Is it time to look for a different workplace that is more attuned to your Personal Mission Statement?

- What other factors might need some tweaking? For example, if you work in a small business and you're getting tired of interpersonal dramas that often come with that kind of environment, you may want to look for a job in a bigger company where there might be less intensity.

Side Hustle

Unless you're independently wealthy, you most likely need a flow of income to keep a roof over your head and food on the table. You may have a family to take care of as well. You might have large student loan debt that you're still paying off. There could be a number of reasons why you can't afford to take the risk involved with making a Big Leap.

One low-risk way to experiment with work that expresses more of your Core Intention is to create a Side Hustle. (That's a great name for a dance step, isn't it? I wish I could take credit for it but it's actually a career-related term that's been around for a while.) The beauty of a Side Hustle is that you can keep your current job, or some form of it, as you experiment. The Side Hustle may actually turn into full-time work at some point, but it affords you the stability of your current income while you nurture a new possibility.

Side Hustles have been the source of some of my most fulfilling work, even if the money they generated was small (or nonexistent). Some of my Side Hustles have included coordinating mindfulness retreats, starting a blog, and creating the online program that eventually evolved into the book you're holding in your hands. In each case, I set aside the question of "How much money can I make from this?" and instead followed my passion and curiosity. I've been amazed at how they have evolved. I wouldn't have imagined that my interest in meditation would eventually become the centerpiece of my work, but volunteering to coordinate mindfulness retreats many years ago started me on that path.

Lyndon, whom you've met before in this book, is another great example of someone who successfully mastered a Side Hustle. His primary livelihood is chaplaincy, and he teaches yoga as well. Recently, Lyndon started creating products for beard care that he sells on an Etsy store called Bearded Yogi. How in the world does all that connect? Well, here is Lyndon's Core Intention:

Helping to end suffering in other people, whether that's mental, physical, or spiritual—that's when I feel most alive, useful, satisfied.

Now listen to his story:

I often ended my yoga classes by placing scented eye pillows on my students for the final relaxation time called savasana. After class people often said that the last few minutes was the most relaxed they had felt in ages and always asked me about the scent of the pillows. It just made sense to incorporate that calming and rejuvenating fragrance into the perfect beard oil.

It's pretty good stuff and it's fun to make it and sell it. It's just play money right now, but the fact that I can make it and even come out in the black is great! I don't think I ever would have started it if I hadn't gotten to that point of seeing that making a lot of money shouldn't be the point of doing something. When you get rid of that motivation, you have a lot more options on the table than you thought you did.

If you're intrigued by the idea of dancing a Side Hustle, here are some starting points:

- What activities bring you joy and are related to your Core Intention, even if you can't imagine how they could make you money? Some possibilities are nature photography, coaching your daughter's basketball team, creating opportunities for young people to express themselves through art, baking cookies, hanging out with alpacas.
- How can you turn this activity into a money-making opportunity? Some Side Hustles may start as volunteer or no-income gigs, but can evolve into income-generating activities. For example, photography may begin as a hobby, but you can let friends know you're available to take photos of their graduations or other special events and that you'd welcome donations so you can purchase better equipment.
- How can you carve out more time in your schedule to experiment with a Side Hustle? It doesn't have to take much—sometimes just a few hours a week is enough to launch a project and if you feel excited about it, it doesn't even feel like "work." But as the name implies, it does take "hustle" so be prepared to put time and energy into it.

Big Leap

You may be eagerly awaiting the description for this dance step. A Big Leap seems so … exciting, so sexy! It could mean launching your own business or starting out in a brand-new professional field. Sometimes a Big Leap is a way to reboot your life, like moving to an ashram for a year or traveling around the world or going to graduate school to prepare for a new career. You may be clear that you need to get out of a toxic work environment but beyond that you have only a vague idea of what your next step is.

An impulsive and unplanned Big Leap may be just what you need *and* there may be risks involved. This is why people often avoid them.

It can take a while to recover financially when you change from one profession to another, and it also takes time to build credibility and relationships in your new field. However, with some planning, you can take steps that allow for a more easeful transition. In fact all of the above dance steps are excellent ways to prepare yourself for a Big Leap.

Two of my Big Leaps were rather harrowing. The first, when I left my career as a mental health professional and went to graduate school for anthropology, was born from burnout and desperation. The second was involuntary when I was laid off from my job with a San Francisco Bay Area nonprofit and then started my own business. Both felt like jumping off a cliff without knowing what would be at the bottom. In the case of the layoff, it felt more like being pushed off a cliff. The upside? I *had* to figure out how to make my business succeed. It's amazing how resourceful you can be when failure isn't an option.

I'm currently in the midst of another Big Leap, shifting from nonprofit consulting to spending more time teaching meditation retreats, facilitating workshops, and offering spiritual mentorship. This leap is just as gratifying as the previous ones but not as terrifying. What's made the difference? Here are four factors:

- My **Personal Mission Statement** has a served as a reassuring reference point. Because I've taken the time to understand my Core Intention and prioritize it when looking for jobs and creating my own work, the results are much more attuned with my mission and I'm clearer on the direction I'm headed.
- **Side Hustles** have helped to build a foundation for this Big Leap. Over the past few years, I've maintained my consulting practice with nonprofits in order to bring in a steady stream of income. At the same time, I collaborated with a friend to create an online program called "Waking Up to Your Life" that supports people who want to start or deepen a contemplative practice. In addition, I facilitated a number of in-person workshops and retreats. The income from these activities hasn't

been enough to fully support me financially, but it's gradually increasing. Most importantly, these Side Hustles have given me a chance to explore this new area and practice my skills as a teacher, and they have been very fulfilling because they're so aligned with my personal mission.

- I have a **Freedom Fund** that equals approximately three months of my expenses. I can draw on this fund during times when my income takes a dip, which gives me more latitude to try new things without going into a financial panic.
- My ability to **ask for support** has greatly improved as I've gotten more clarity on what I'm asking for and more comfortable reaching out to people who might be willing and able to offer support. Over the last few years, I've made a practice of writing a letter or posting on Facebook to let people know what I have to offer. As a result of these outreach efforts, some wonderful opportunities have manifested including several new nonprofit clients as well as an invitation to contribute a chapter to a book on mindfulness. But they wouldn't have happened if I hadn't asked. Check out the Appendix for a sample "Treasure Hunting" letter you can use when you're ready to put out a call for support to your community of friends, colleagues, and potential employers or clients.

Finally, it's worth noting the issues of healthcare and insurance as factors that might deter you from taking a Big Leap. It's important to make sure that your basic needs, including healthcare, are taken care of before you make a change in your work situation that may result in you losing insurance coverage, particularly if you have a chronic medical condition. Readers in Canada, Australia, New Zealand, and European and Asian countries with socialized health care don't have to deal with this, but if you're in the US, it's a real consideration.

As of the writing of this book, the Affordable Care Act or ACA (also known as "Obamacare") is still in effect in the United States, though its fate is unclear. The ACA provides health insurance coverage for people without employer-sponsored insurance. Prior to the ACA, health insurance was tied to your job (if you were lucky enough to have an employer who provided it as a benefit). The ACA makes it possible for people to take their insurance coverage with them when changing from one employer to another, or when becoming self-employed.

Regardless of what happens with the ACA, don't give up your dreams. It's still possible to get creative about how you meet this need. Many associations or guilds offer their members the option to purchase health insurance through group plans. One example is the Freelancers Union (www.freelancersunion.org). Another avenue to explore are community clinics that provide low-cost or free healthcare to those who meet income requirements. While universal healthcare may not be the norm in the US, it is possible to find pockets of progressive policy and services in some states and cities. For example, the Commonwealth of Massachusetts has established a public authority to facilitate the purchase of health insurance; the Oregon Health Plan has created Coordinated Care Organizations to serve citizens of that state; and the city of San Francisco subsidizes medical care for the uninsured. If you happen to be sixty-five or older, you are eligible for Medicare.

If you're feeling like a Big Leap is what you need and yet it feels overwhelming, these dance steps are useful reminders that you're not limited to an all-or-nothing choice.

I admit, I'm biased—of all the pathways I've been on, this third one has brought me the most fulfillment and happiness, even when it's been challenging. Let's close this chapter with a taste of how exhilarating it can feel to create your own work. This story comes from Sam, a Fall in Love with Your Work graduate, who has been joyously experimenting with her own livelihood formulation:

> *A couple of years ago, I was in a place where my gut was telling me I could absolutely find a way to bridge my passions of health, well-being, and creative engagement with my work experience in film production management. My intent was to turn this into an income.*
>
> *I had years of meditation and yoga practice. I had over two decades of experience in film/TV production but did not want to work in scripted drama anymore. I knew I could produce, but produce what? It had to matter. The year previous, I experienced an internal creative explosion, so I burst forth and filmed some pieces that contributed to the puzzle of what I wanted to create, but everything was blurry and confused for what seemed the longest time. I just didn't know how I wanted it to come together and what I really had to offer.*
>
> *After going through Fall in Love with Your Work and receiving some individual coaching from Maia, the ideas are*

now becoming structured possibilities. With a vision and mission in place, I am creating content for New Moon Journey, a project comprised of a monthly New Moon Newsletter to a growing community of enthusiasts offering resources and personal experience with holistic health, contemplative well-being, and creative engagement. I am researching and developing content for my website, www.newmoonjourney.com, intended to offer encouragement and motivation for people to engage in these areas in their daily lives. I am currently interviewing, writing, and editing profile articles of artists, yogis, nutritionists, and Indigenous Canadians doing important, impactful work. I'm pursuing funding and learning business strategies to produce visionary content about the inspiring movers and shakers of the global spiritual community whose work is desperately needed at this time.

I am determined and well on my way to shaping a small business and creative project that services individuals and small groups and I am passionate about producing content to inspire and inform. I feel like my tiny empire is finally coming together!

QUESTIONS FOR REFLECTION

Here are some questions to ask yourself to help you evaluate where you are in the dance of work:

- Am I ready for a Big Leap? Or is that more risk than I'm willing to take right now?
- If I'm in Glide mode, how can I use this time to prepare for a Big Leap?
- Would a Pivot serve me right now? What might that look like?
- What kind of Side Hustle could bring more meaning, purpose, and joy to my work life? And also help to prepare me for a Big Leap?

CHAPTER 12 Create Your Personal Action Plan

The plan (on the next page) has three sections:

1. The Big Picture—to keep you moving toward your long-term goal related to Liberation-Based Livelihood.
2. My Promise to Myself—to help you focus on one Action Area, choose tasks related to it, and set a time line.
3. Keeping it Real—to increase your follow-through by building accountability into the process.

Detailed instructions for each section are included after the worksheet.

This is important: Please don't set yourself up to become overwhelmed. When you start filling out the second section, please choose only *one* Action Area and a task or two within it to include on your plan. Then focus on it intensely for a period of time that you designate—a week, a month, or whatever time frame feels doable to you. This alone can result in a big shift.

You can reuse this worksheet as many times as you'd like. For example, you might choose to "Start or Grow Your Freedom Fund" during the next month. After that you can use the worksheet again to focus on "Building Your Presence."

Keep it simple. You'll have the best chance of success if you set your intention on making one thing actually happen rather than taking on too much.

"WORK THAT MATTERS" MY PERSONAL ACTION PLAN

Date:

A) THE BIG PICTURE: MY PERSONAL MISSION STATEMENT:
My goal: In the next [week/month/year or whatever time frame feels right to you] I will...

B) MY PROMISE TO MYSELF
To get me closer to my goal, the Action Area I will focus on right now is:

These are the steps that I promise to take:
1) I will:

Target date to complete this step:
2) I will:

Target date to complete this step:
3) I will:

Target date to complete this step:

C) KEEPING IT REAL
I will share this plan with _____ and hold myself accountable by giving them updates about my progress every _____ [week, month, etc.].

Feel free to use other sheets of paper for notes, lists of people and resources that can help you carry out your steps, things you may need to let go of or stop in order to do this, and anything else that comes up!

SECTION A: THE BIG PICTURE

Start by writing in the Personal Mission Statement you've come up with so far. If you have more than one, choose just one for each Action Plan you create.

Then, give yourself a goal that is related to the vision you've described in your Personal Mission Statement. Your goal should be big enough that this feels like a stretch and yet is still within the realm of possibility. Here are some examples:

- I will leave my current job and find another in my field that is more fulfilling and in alignment with my values.
- I will start a Side Hustle that will pave the way for leaving my job.
- I will start my own blog on the topic of mindful parenting.
- I will start my own business making gourmet toffee candy from my home.
- I will start a nonprofit organization that serves underprivileged children in my community.
- I will spend six months volunteering with an international development organization in Ecuador.
- I will live at a spiritual retreat center for a year.

Putting your goal down on paper doesn't mean that you're obligated to make it happen in an unrealistic amount of time, only that you're committing yourself to steps that will bring it closer to fruition. As you consistently take enough of these small steps, your goal will become possible.

SECTION B: MY PROMISE TO MYSELF

In this section, choose one of the following four Action Areas, which will bring you closer to your goal. I've included examples of smaller steps under each one. Feel free to add any of them in your Action Plan or come up with others that are relevant for you. Make sure to set a time line for each one. Again, in the spirit of simplicity, I encourage you to choose no more than three steps. That's plenty! Set yourself up for success, not overwhelm and frustration.

ACTION AREA 1: START OR GROW YOUR FREEDOM FUND

A Freedom Fund is a savings account that strengthens your financial stability so that you feel more free to take risks in the area of livelihood. If you already have such a fund, that's fantastic. Keep adding to it and set a goal around how much you want to grow it. If you don't, start now.

Give yourself a concrete goal for Section A, e.g., "I will start my Freedom Fund this month and deposit at least one hundred dollars a month in it from now on."

As a general rule, a Freedom Fund should provide you with enough money to cover at least **three months** of your basic expenses. If you don't know this number, take time to add up all of the following to get your monthly amount:

- housing (rent or mortgage)
- utilities (phone, electricity, gas, etc.)
- groceries
- transportation (including auto insurance)
- healthcare (including insurance)
- childcare
- debt (student loan and other regular payments)

It's okay if you come up with an estimate. This doesn't need to be an exact number, but you do want to have a sense of how much you need each month to take care of your basic financial needs. You will have other nonessential expenses such as vacations, movies, dining out, and more. You can consider how you might cut back on these if your financial situation gets tight.

Here are some examples of steps that can save or make you money, which you can then deposit into your Freedom Fund. Small amounts will add up to big numbers over the course of a year.

- Set up an automatic deposit from your paycheck to your Freedom Fund each month. Set aside as much as you can without cutting into the rest of your budget.
- If you dine out a lot, can you make just one less trip to a restaurant each week and cook at home instead? If you save twenty dollars a week there, you've just found eighty dollars a month.
- Check your cable TV bill. Do you really need all those channels? Making some reductions on this expense might save you twenty dollars or more each month.
- Look at your auto insurance and consider if you can reduce your premium by choosing a higher deductible or making other adjustments.
- Review everything that you've put on auto payment: magazine subscriptions, software, etc. Can you discontinue any of those services?

- Get rid of all that stuff you don't need and sell it at a yard sale or on Craigslist. This can easily add up to a couple of hundred dollars.
- If you have an extra bedroom in your house or apartment, consider renting it out or putting it on Airbnb for occasional vacation rentals. This could bring in a hundred to five hundred dollars a month … or more.
- If you live in a metropolitan area, check out Task Rabbit (www.taskrabbit.com) or another casual job-finding app. You can sign up to provide a service such as cleaning, delivery, or personal assistant work and you choose your rates and hours. Nice deal! Or you can post an ad offering your services on a bulletin board in your local grocery store or coffee shop. Let people know what you can do for them. You may be surprised at how valuable your help is.

ACTION AREA 2 INNER DEVELOPMENT

Remember the 6 Keys? In my experience, we can learn all kinds of skills but if we haven't developed one or more of these Keys, we may sabotage our success. For example, if you don't value yourself, you may not believe that you are deserving of an extraordinary work opportunity and you'll let it slip by.

Are there one or two Keys that you've discovered you want (and perhaps need) to cultivate? Take a look back at Part 2 of this book for plenty of steps to develop each of these:

- Become Intimate with Your Core Intention
- Value Your Gifts and Time
- Break Through Inertia and Take Action
- Make Friends with Uncertainty
- Think Big and Make the Most of Your Resources
- Build a Circle of Allies and Ask for Help

ACTION AREA 3: SKILL/KNOWLEDGE DEVELOPMENT

This Action Area is about identifying and developing specific skills and knowledge areas that will nurture your Liberation-Based Livelihood. Depending on your professional field, you may need formal training at a college or university. Then there are more general skills, such as time management, that will serve you no matter what your profession and which you can teach yourself or get training in less formal ways. I've listed some of these below along with sample steps.

These days you have so many choices about *how* to learn: books, continuing education classes, online courses, YouTube videos, individual coaching, and much more. All require an investment of your time, some may require a financial investment, but that doesn't mean they have to be expensive. Remember—you are worth it (Key 2)!

Time Management

When you switch from working for someone else to running your own business, you quickly discover how important it is to be mindful and efficient with your time. This is a great skill to strengthen even if you aren't self-employed. Here are some steps to consider:

- Read *The Power of Full Engagement: Managing Energy, Not Time, Is the Key to High Performance and Personal Renewal* (Tony Schwartz and Jim Loehr, 2003, Free Press).
- Read *Getting Things Done: The Art of Stress-Free Productivity* (David Allen, 2015, Penguin).
- Download free planning calendars and other resources from this helpful website: www.productiveflourishing.com/ free-planners/.

Money/Financial Management

After graduate school, I had accumulated more than eighty thousand dollars of total debt, including student loans. This was my wake-up call to get more savvy about how I handled my money, and also to understand the importance of having a Freedom Fund. It took me ten years, but I paid off most of my debt, and I chalk that up to developing more awareness and discipline around the way I relate to money. If your financial habits (or lack of them) are obstructing your capacity to create a Liberation-Based Livelihood, here are some suggested steps to address the inner and outer dimensions of money:

- Read *The Art of Money: A Life-Changing Guide to Financial Happiness* by Bari Tessler (2016, Parallax Press) to gain an all-round understanding of how to create a budget and plan financially for the future. (Bari also runs a year-long Art of Money online program; learn more at her website, baritessler.com/art-of-money/.)
- If you're a freelancer or contractor, read *The Money Book for Freelancers, Part-Timers, and the Self-Employed: The Only Personal*

Finance System for People with Not-So-Regular Jobs by Joseph D'Agrese and Denise Kiernan (2010, Crown Business).

- If you are an entrepreneurial type and have (or dream of having) a business of your own, take a course on basic book-keeping at your community college.

Building Your Presence

Whether you're self-employed or seeking just the right job, you can make it easier for potential clients and employers to find you and understand what you have to offer. Another term for this is "marketing." Perhaps you associate the word with coercion and manipulation, as we are all subjected to a daily bombardment of ads and messages trying to sell us everything under the sun. It's true that many individuals and businesses use marketing tactics to sell us things we don't need or want. However, in its most basic form, marketing is simply the process by which you connect with the people who will most benefit from what you have to offer. When it's done with integrity, marketing is kind of like heavenly matchmaking and everyone wins—the person, organization, or business that truly needs and appreciates your skills, and you.

Here are a number of steps to consider adding to your Personal Action Plan for building your presence:

- Join a Toastmasters group. This peer feedback group model has been around since 1924 and helped thousands of people to improve their public speaking skills.
- Practice telling your story. Find a friend (or two) and ask them to listen as you share your mission statement and your vision of Liberation-Based Livelihood. Ask for their feedback. What about your story intrigues them? What's missing that might make it more compelling? You could even consider signing up for an improv class to learn a new way of communicating, and have fun in the process.
- Build your online platform—a space where people can get to know who you are and what you offer. This often takes the form of a website, but it also could be a podcast channel or social media. Within this step are a number of other steps:
  - Reserve a website domain name.
  - Create a website for yourself and your business.
  - Once you have a domain name and web hosting for your business, set up an email account for your business that

is separate from your personal email. For example, start using mary@bestcandy.com instead mary.smith@hotmail.com.

> » Learn how to effectively use social media (like Facebook, LinkedIn, Twitter, Instagram) to share news about what you're doing and build a base of supporters. If you don't have a Facebook page, set one up.
> » Start a YouTube channel. Create a video about your work and post it on your YouTube channel.

- Set up an email list using a service like MailChimp so that you can start collecting the names of people who like what you're doing and want to hear more from you.
- Design a business card for yourself (or find a graphic designer to do this for you), and bring it with you to conferences and other events where you'll meet potential employers or clients. You might also want to create a brochure to visually communicate the services you offer. We live in an age when it's essential to have a digital presence, but that doesn't mean that old-school communication vehicles are obsolete. A warm handshake and a well-designed business card are still some of the most effective ways to connect with others.
- Begin to collect testimonials and raves. What good things are people saying about you and your work? (You may already have some of these from the 360-Degree Survey you did back in Key 5.) As your collection of these endorsements grows, you can include them on your website and brochure.

Skills Unique to Your Situation

For example, if your goal is to make toffee candy out of your home kitchen and sell it at your local farmer's market, check to see what's required for this to become a reality. You may need to take a course in commercial cooking and food safety at your community college. Put that step on your plan when the time is right.

ACTION AREA 4: REVENUE CREATION

Getting paid for what you do is a wonderful feeling! Even early on, you can take steps to create income or make it possible to receive income sooner rather than later. Here are some steps to plug into your Personal Action Plan if you're ready to focus on Revenue Creation:

- Create a way to receive money. Set up an account with PayPal or a similar service. Open up a separate checking account for your new business.
- Put a PayPal donation button on your website and invite people to support you.
- Consider an area of expertise that you have and let people know that you're now available for consulting on that topic. We often get hung up on thinking we need more training or some kind of certification to do this, but this usually isn't the case (with the exception of some health and legal areas). Think about it. Do you have a knack for finding fantastic outfits at thrift stores? You could start a business selling clothes on eBay, ThredUp, or other online clothing sites. Or you could offer your services on a one-to-one basis for busy people who want to dress well on a budget but have no idea how to find treasures among the trash. Do you love to share community resources with people? You could start an online neighborhood newsletter and generate revenue through advertisements from local businesses. Do friends often ask you for help to organize their papers and filing systems? New jobs could include running a professional decluttering service or being an office assistant. All of these skills (and more) can be turned into income-generating work.
- Turn your craft into an income. If you're an artist or craftsperson, open up an Etsy account and put your first product up for sale. If you're a writer, self-publish your work and offer it for sale, or look for paid writing gigs in your field of interest.
- Share your vision with your community and invite them to support you and your project. Create a campaign on Indiegogo, Kickstarter, Patreon, or other crowdfunding platforms.
- If you have a blog that is beginning to grow in popularity, invite compatible individuals or businesses to sponsor your site.

SECTION C: KEEPING IT REAL

The chances that you'll follow through with the promises you made in Section B, My Promise to Myself, increase when you have someone who helps to hold you accountable. Back in chapter 3, I suggested that you choose an "accountability buddy" as you go through this book. If you did that, you could ask this same person to serve in that role for your Personal Action Plan. If you haven't found someone, think about whom you can invite to support you in this process. Who has your best interests at heart and wants to see you be happy in your work? It could be a friend, a former colleague, or a family member. Once you find that person, make sure you specify how often you'll check in with them. If your accountability buddy is also going through a similar transition, you can support each other as you both find work that matters.

A beautiful option is to start a "learning community" based on this book. Invite a small group of people who are also searching for work that matters and use this book as your collective study and practice guide. You can meet at a regular frequency, like once a month, as a way to support each other's progress. You'll find tips on how to structure this group on my website: maiaduerr.com/work-that-matters. In spiritual traditions, people recognize that individuals need a group of like-minded friends around them to make progress on the path toward liberation; in our journey toward freedom from toxic work habits and cultures, building a community around meaningful work can be one of the most nourishing acts you can do for yourself.

CONCLUSION True Freedom through Work That Matters

As I write the last pages of this book, the outcome of the 2016 US presidential elections has touched down like a political and psychic tornado, turning the country and our global community upside down. As you pick up this book, dear reader, I have no idea what kind of world we will be living in. Perhaps this new administration will succeed in strengthening the economy and creating opportunities for new jobs. Perhaps the volatility that has rocked our world will continue, creating conditions for economic instability. The only thing that is certain is that change is a constant truth.

The economy is always an invisible force that drives the decisions we make, especially those related to our livelihood. In times of economic and political stability, it's easier to take risks like leaving an unfulfilling job and seeking a new one or starting a business. And yet, there are hidden openings in periods such as this. As a brilliant friend of mine who teaches complexity theory says, on the edge of chaos anything is possible.

We live in a time when the oppressive aspects of institutions such as capitalism and patriarchy are becoming increasingly and painfully clear. I believe that we're in a collective birthing process, with the emergence of more life-giving and sustainable forms of relating to each other and the planet. But just as all birthing processes are marked by expansions and contractions, this one will no doubt be messy (and already is).

My awareness of what it takes to create work that truly matters, and developing the Keys and practices to make it come to fruition, grew out of a similar chaotic period in 2008 as the rotting pillars of the US economy began to collapse. That crisis gave rise to an unexpected job loss for me. So much of my identity was wrapped up in that job that it felt like I lost a part of myself. The economic impact was huge as well; I can still remember sending out one résumé after another, and growing increasingly nervous as I heard nothing back. Yet all of this turned out to be a blessing in disguise as I set off on a path of creative self-employment. The eight years of relative economic stability that followed allowed me to experiment with some of the innovative forms of work that I've described in this book.

When I entered that accelerated phase of creating work that matters, I did it because I had to. I didn't have the luxury of making a choice about it. While my work draws on some traditional business practices, I've deviated from conventional advice and improvise a lot. My meditation practice has informed a great deal of the way I approached my business. It gives me clarity on where fear and doubt are stopping me, and it keeps me connected to my Core Intention.

To this day, I am able to sustain myself, yet my business is not hugely "profitable" on a strictly financial level. That's okay with me. I don't own a home. My car is nearly twenty years old (and I dream of not having a car and returning to public transportation). I don't have a television, and my phone is decidedly not "smart." (I do allow myself the luxury of a mini iPad.) Most of my clothes and furniture come from secondhand stores.

I've consciously chosen a simple lifestyle in order to stay focused on what brings me joy, and to be able to take on clients who may not be able to pay the highest fees but whose values align with my own. This is in alignment with my spiritual values as well as my livelihood. These may not be choices you want to make, but the point is to consider your own priorities and values, and then calibrate your actions to them in a way that makes sense for you.

While my lifestyle may seem austere, I am rich in so many other ways. I have cultivated my inner resources, my resourcefulness, and my circle of allies so I don't have to be so dependent on conventional measures of success or wealth. My livelihood was designed to be nimble in the face of loss and chaos, because that's the ferment from which it was born during that 2008 tailspin.

What I know without a doubt is that the same qualities that I had to develop and deepen then will serve you well in our present times:

- The capacity, through contemplative practice, to know yourself and your Core Intention.
- The capacity to understand your inherent gifts and to become fiercely protective of them, as a mother would be of her children.
- The capacity to channel that clarity around your Core Intention and your gifts and use it to dissolve whatever might be blocking you from acting on them.
- The capacity to work productively with your fears so you can leverage the energy within them in a positive and proactive direction.
- The capacity to imagine great things for yourself and your work, even if you do them in humble ways; the capacity to redefine "resources" beyond the financial.
- The capacity to grow your community in a heartfelt and reciprocal way, knowing without a doubt that a rising tide lifts all boats.

You've arrived at the end of this book, but I know that your journey to create work that matters will continue for the rest of your life. If you return to the process in this book at another point in time, I can almost guarantee that you'll have a new experience and you'll uncover more aspects of yourself. I appreciate this reflection that Katya shared about her journey to create a Liberation-Based Livelihood:

> *I have taken Fall in Love with Your Work twice, and each time was an incredible opportunity. The first time around I felt quite lost. I had recently left my job as a hospice social worker and*

was asking questions such as, "What is my purpose here on this planet?" "How can I find fulfillment in the work I do as well as serve others?" and "How can I support myself so that I can support others?"

The course helped me to focus, set my intentions, and find more clarity in terms of the "what" and the "how."

When I took the course the second time, I was able to explore with a different perspective, a broader view. I wasn't as lost. I had more confidence in exploring what Liberated-Based Livelihood is, and did not so easily fall back into the mind-set I carried of needing to have a "real job." I was able to recognize that a nine-to-five job is not for me and that I was not a failure for not being able to fit into that way of life. It reminds me of how I recognized that everyone learns differently and that in fact I was not "stupid" because I didn't learn the way I was taught in public schools.

Now I understand that I am not taking a path that is already laid out, but rather I am discovering it as I go. I have deepened my practice of trusting that I am right where I need to be. I continue to learn about myself and often refer back to my notes from the course. I have a feeling that this is a lifetime exploration.

As we come to the end of this segment of the journey, my wish is that you recognize what has the greatest value in your life and that you commit to giving it more of your time and energy. I hope that this book has helped you learn some great dance moves to make this possible. And I hope that the practices in these pages have supported you to break through some of the limiting thoughts and beliefs you may have been carrying about yourself and what your work can look like.

I would love to hear your story as you go through this process, and I'd like to introduce you to others who share the same intention to create work that matters. Please stay in touch through the maiaduerr.com/work-that-matters website and be part of our ongoing community of learning and practice.

NOTES

E. F. Schumacher, Ellen Schwartz, and Suzanne Stoddard, *Taking Back Our Lives in an Age of Corporate Dominance* (San Francisco, CA: Berrett-Koehler Publishers, 1999), p. 140.

CHAPTER 1

Marge Piercy, "To Be of Use" from *Circles on the Water: Selected Poems of Marge Piercy* (New York: Knopf, 1982).

1. Anya Kamenetz, "The Four Year Career," *Fast Company*, February 2012, http://www.fastcompany.com/1802731/four-year-career.

2. Pamela Slim, *Body of Work: Finding the Thread That Ties Your Story Together* (New York: Portfolio, 2013), p. 4.

CHAPTER 2

Thich Nhat Hanh, *The Heart of the Buddha's Teaching: Transforming Suffering into Peace, Joy, and Liberation* (New York: Broadway Books, 1999).

3. Christina Pazzanese, "The High Price of Workplace Stress," *Harvard Gazette*, July 12, 2016, http://news.harvard.edu/gazette/story/2016/07/the-high-price-of-workplace-stress.

4. Anita Roddick, "Dispatch: Reflections on Success, Part 1," AnitaRoddick.com, September 9, 2003, http://www.anitaroddick.com/readmore.php?sid=154.

5. Robert Safian, "This is Generation Flux: Meet the Pioneers of the New (and Chaotic) Frontier of Business," January 9, 2012, http://www.fastcompany.com/1802732/generation-flux-meet-pioneers-new-and-chaotic-frontier-business.

CHAPTER 4

6. Adyashanti, *The Way of Liberation: A Practical Guide to Spiritual Enlightenment* (Open Gate Sangha, 2013), p. xi.

7. Peters, Kim, Michelle K. Ryan, and S. Alexander Haslam. "Marines, medics, and machismo: Lack of fit with masculine occupational stereotypes discourages men's participation." *British Journal of Psychology* 106, no. 4 (2015): 635–655.

CHAPTER 5

8. Elizabeth Gilbert, Facebook post from Nov 2014.

9. Belinda Luscombe, "Do We Need $75,000 a Year to Be Happy?" *Time*, September 6, 2010, http://content.time.com/time/magazine/article/0,9171,2019628,00.html.

10. John P. Kotter, "To Create Healthy Urgency, Focus on a Big Opportunity," *Harvard Business Review*, February 21, 2014, https://hbr.org/2014/02/to-create-healthy-urgency-focus-on-a-big-opportunity.

11. "The Three Tenets of the Zen Peacemakers," accessed August 19, 2017, http://zenpeacemakers.org/2013/03/the-three-tenets-of-the-zen-peacemakers/.

12. Roshi Bernie Glassman, "Harvard Divinity School Lectures (Fall 2007), Lecture 3 – Bearing Witness," *Zen Peacemakers*, October 1, 2007, http://zenpeacemakers.org/who-we-are__trashed/zen-peacemakers-sangha__trashed/dharma-talks__trashed/bernie-divinity-lecture-3/.

13. Eve Ensler, *Insecure at Last: A Political Memoir* (New York: Villard, 2007), p. xiii.

CHAPTER 8

Marianne Williamson, *A Return to Love* (San Francisco: HarperOne, 1996), p. 190.

14. Eva Pereira, "The Role Model Effect: Women Leaders Key to Inspiring the Next Generation." Jan 19, 2012, Forbes.com. https://www.forbes.com/sites/worldviews/2012/01/19/the-role-model-effect-women-leaders-key-to-inspiring-the-next-generation/#7d67cf2a4fd2

15. If you're interested in learning more about how gender informs our experience of the world, *In a Different Voice: Psychological Theory and Women's Development* by Carol Gilligan (Harvard University Press, 2016) is a wonderful and essential book on this topic.

16. Lynne Twist, "How Much is Enough? Embracing the Concept of Sufficiency," *Economica: Women and the Global Economy*, accessed August 19, 2017, http://exhibitions.globalfundforwomen.org/economica/giving/how-much-is-enough.

17. David Spangler, *Everyday Miracles: The Inner Art of Manifestation* (New York: Bantam, 1996) and http://www.co-intelligence.org/P-Spangler.html.

18. Rob Brezsny, *Pronoia Is the Antidote for Paranoia* (Berkeley, CA: North Atlantic Books, 2005), p. 248.

19. Nicholas Christakis, and James Fowler, "The spread of obesity in a large social network over 32 years." *New England Journal of Medicine*, July 26, 2007; 357(4):370–9. Epub July 25, 2007.

20. Rob Stein, "Obesity Spreads in Social Circles as Trends Do, Study Indicates," *The Washington Post,* July 26, 2007, http://www.washingtonpost.com/wp-dyn/content/article/2007/07/25/AR2007072501353.html.

21. Sarah Van Gelder, *The Revolution Where You Live: Stories from a 12,000-Mile Journey Through a New America* (San Francisco: Berrett-Koehler Publishers, 2017), p. 94.

22. Chris Guillebeau, *The $100 Startup: Reinvent the Way You Make a Living, Do What You Love, and Create a New Future* (New York: Crown Business, 2012), p. 46.

23. Britt Reints, "How to Write a Mission Statement (and Why I Bothered)," *In Pursuit of Happiness,* accessed August 19, 2017, http://inpursuitofhappiness.net/blog/2012/05/16/how-to-write-a-mission-statement-and-why-i-bothered.

24. Tracy Cochran, "The Pentagon Meditation Club," *Parabola,* December 10, 2015, https://parabola.org/2015/12/10/the-pentagon-meditation-club-by-tracy-cochran/.

25. Scott Dinsmore, "Why Chris Guillebeau Believes a Startup is Less Risky than a Corporate Job + His Best Alternative," *Live Your Legend,* June 11, 2012, http://liveyourlegend.net/chris-guillebeau-non-risky-100-startup/.

26. "Contingent Work Force: Size, Characteristics, Earnings, and Benefits," U.S. Government Accountability Office, April 20, 2015, http://www.gao.gov/assets/670/669899.pdf.

RESOURCES

You can find an updated and expanded list of resources on the Work That Matters website: www.maiaduerr.com/work-that-matters.

CHAPTER 3: BUILDING BLOCKS OF TRANSFORMATION
MINDFULNESS PRACTICE: SUGGESTED READING

Nhat Hanh, Thich. *Being Peace*. Berkeley, CA: Parallax Press, 2005.

Nhat Hanh, Thich. *How to Sit*. Berkeley, CA: Parallax Press, 2014.

Nhat Hanh, Thich. *How to Walk*. Berkeley, CA: Parallax Press, 2015.

Salgado, Brenda, ed. *Real World Mindfulness for Beginners: Navigate Daily Life One Practice at a Time*. Berkeley, CA: Sonoma Press, 2016.

Salzberg, Sharon. *Lovingkindness: The Revolutionary Art of Happiness*. Boulder, CO: Shambhala Classics, 2002.

ONLINE PROGRAM

Waking Up to Your Life with Maia Duerr and Katya Lesher: www.maiaduerr.com/waking-up-to-your-life/.

LEVERAGING ADVERSITY: SUGGESTED READING

Steindl-Rast, Brother David. *A Good Day: A Gift of Gratitude*. New York: Sterling Ethos, 2014.

WEBSITE

www.gratefulness.org.

STAYING THE COURSE: SUGGESTED READING

Loehr, Jim, and Tony Schwartz. *The Power of Full Engagement: Managing Energy, Not Time, Is the Key to High Performance and Personal Renewal*. New York: Free Press, 2003.

CHAPTER 4: BECOMING INTIMATE WITH YOUR CORE INTENTION
SUGGESTED READING

Rockwell, Irini. *The Five Wisdom Energies: A Buddhist Way of Understanding Personality, Emotions, and Relationships*. Boulder, CO: Shambhala, 2002.

Slim, Pamela. *Body of Work: Finding the Thread That Ties Your Story Together*. New York: Portfolio, 2013.

ONLINE ASSESSMENT TOOLS

Character Strengths Survey from VIA Institute of Character (free)
www.viacharacter.org
This free and simple self-assessment can help you to understand your core characteristics, the positive parts of your personality that impact how you think, feel, and behave. The Character Strengths Survey takes between ten and fifteen minutes to complete.

Personal Values Assessment from the Barrett Values Centre (free)
www.valuescentre.com/our-products/products-individuals/personal-values-assessment-pva
This free test takes about five minutes to complete and will give you helpful clues about the values that are most important to you.

Clifton StrengthsFinder from Gallup Strengths Center
www.gallupstrengthscenter.com.

This assessment helps you to identify your talents and gives you a way to develop your unique combination of skills, talents, and knowledge. You can choose from the basic version for fifteen dollars to discover your top five strengths; the next level is seventy-four dollars and identifies between six and thirty-four strengths along with more detailed information on how to establish strategies for maximizing your talents.

CHAPTER 5: VALUE YOUR GIFTS AND TIME
SUGGESTED READING

Neff, Kristin. *Self-Compassion: The Proven Power of Being Kind to Yourself.* New York: William Morrow Paperbacks, 2015.

Tessler, Bari. *The Art of Money: A Life-Changing Guide to Financial Happiness.* Berkeley, CA: Parallax Press, 2016.

Ury, William. *The Power of a Positive No: Save the Deal, Save the Relationship—And Still Say No.* New York: Bantam, 2007.

CHAPTER 6: BREAK THROUGH INERTIA AND TAKE ACTION
SUGGESTED READING

Dutton, Indigo Ocean. *Micro Habits for Major Happiness: Everything You Need to Build True Success, One Easy Step at a Time.* El Cerrito, CA: Bodhi Press, 2014.

Tracy, Brian. *Eat That Frog! 21 Great Ways to Stop Procrastinating and Get More Done in Less Time.* Oakland, CA: Berrett-Koehler Publishers, 2007.

TOOL

The Pomodoro Timer is a time management technique that can help to boost your productivity. The timer gives you a timed twenty-five-minute period of work followed by a five-minute break. After four work intervals, there is a fifteen-minute break. You can find an online version of the Pomodoro Timer at www.marinaratimer.com, which also includes a custom timer in case you want to adjust the intervals.

CHAPTER 7: MAKE FRIENDS WITH UNCERTAINTY
SUGGESTED READING

Fields, Jonathan. *Uncertainty: Turning Fear and Doubt into Fuel for Brilliance.* New York: Portfolio, 2012.

Gilbert, Elizabeth. *Big Magic: Creative Living Beyond Fear.* New York: Riverhead Books, 2016.

Glassman, Bernie. *Instructions to the Cook: A Zen Master's Lessons on Living a Life That Matters.* Boulder, CO: Shambhala, 2013.

CHAPTER 8: THINK BIG AND MAKE THE MOST OF YOUR RESOURCES
SUGGESTED READING

Eisenstein, Charles. *Sacred Economics: Money, Gift, and Society in the Age of Transition.* Berkeley, CA: Evolver Editions, 2011.

LaPorte, Danielle. *The Desire Map: A Guide to Creating Goals with Soul.* Boulder, CO: Sounds True, 2014.

Spangler, David. *Everyday Miracles: The Inner Art of Manifestation.* New York: Bantam, 1996.

Twist, Lynne. *The Soul of Money: Reclaiming the Wealth of Our Inner Resources.* New York: W. W. Norton & Company, 2006.

CHAPTER 9: BUILD A CIRCLE OF ALLIES AND ASK FOR HELP
SUGGESTED READING

Gilliard, Joyce M. *The Little Book About Toxic Friends: How to Recognize a Toxic Relationship.* Bloomington, IN: Xlibris, 2016.

Palmer, Amanda. *The Art of Asking: How I Learned to Stop Worrying and Let People Help.* New York: Grand Central Publishing, 2015.

Spadaro, Patricia. *Honor Yourself: The Inner Art of Giving and Receiving.* Bozeman, MT: Three Wings Press, 2009.

CHAPTER 10: CRAFTING YOUR PERSONAL MISSION STATEMENT
TOOL

Franklin Covey Mission Statement Builder: https://msb.franklincovey.com.

CHAPTER 11: NAVIGATING THE THREE PATHWAYS
PATHWAY 1: PLAN YOUR EXIT STRATEGY
SUGGESTED READING

Gillet, Rachel, "16 Signs It's Time to Quit Your Job," *Business Insider,* www.businessinsider.com/signs-you-should-quit-your-job-2016-2.

PATHWAY 2: LOVE THE JOB YOU'VE GOT: SUGGESTED READING

Covey, Stephen. *The Seven Habits of Highly Successful People: Powerful Lessons in Personal Change.* New York: Simon & Schuster, 2013.

Gelles, David. *Mindful Work: How Meditation Is Changing Business from the Inside Out.* Boston, MA: Eamon Dolan/Mariner Books, 2016.

Richmond, Lewis. *Work as a Spiritual Practice: A Practical Buddhist Approach to Inner Growth and Satisfaction on the Job.* New York: Harmony: 2000.

Salzberg, Sharon. *Real Happiness at Work: Meditations for Accomplishment, Achievement, and Peace.* New York: Workman Publishing Company, 2013.

HOW TO MAKE A CASE FOR TELECOMMUTING

Nevogt, Dave. "Are Remote Workers More Productive? We've Checked All the Research So You Don't Have To," July 25, 2016. www.blog.hubstaff.com/remote-workers-more-productive.

HOW TO MAKE THE CASE FOR A SALARY INCREASE

Babcock, Linda. *Ask For It: How Women Can Use the Power of Negotiation to Get What They Really Want.* New York: Bantam, 2009.

PATHWAY 3: CREATE WORK THAT YOU LOVE

Expanding Your Sense of Possibilities / The Annotated List

1) International and domestic service opportunities, like the Peace Corps and AmeriCorps, visit www.backdoorjobs.com.

2) Become a resident at an ashram or other spiritual center.

Here are some examples of spiritual centers with robust residential programs:

Breitenbush Hot Springs, Detroit, Oregon breitenbush.com/employment/.

Insight Meditation Society, Barre, Massachuetts www.dharma.org/generosity/volunteering.

Kalani Oceanside Retreat, Pahoa, Hawai'i kalani.com/volunteer.

Mount Madonna Center, Watsonville, California www.mountmadonna.org/programs-retreats/ysc.

Omega Institute, Rhinebeck, New York www.eomega.org/seasonal-community-experience.

The Rowe Center, Rowe, Massachusetts rowecenter.org/wp/volunteer-residency-program/.

Shambhala Mountain Center, Red Feather Lakes, Colorado www.shambhalamountain.org/about/join-our-staff/.

Shivananda Ashram Yoga Farm, Grass Valley, California sivanandayogafarm.org/en/topic/seva-study.

Upaya Zen Center, Santa Fe, New Mexico www.upaya.org/being-at-upaya/residential-program/.

To search for retreat centers in your area, visit www.findthedivine.com
(Keep in mind that not all retreat centers have residential programs.)

3) Become an intern to learn a specific skill.

A comprehensive directory of internship sites is available online here: www.internships.com.

4) **Become a consultant—offer your expertise to companies or organizations.**
The Instant Consultant by Chris Guillebeau: chrisguillebeau.com/the-instant-consultant/.

5) **Teach a group of people a subject that you know well and that they would like to learn.**
Schank, Roger C. *Lessons in Learning, e-Learning, and Training: Perspectives and Guidance for the Enlightened Trainer.* Hoboken, NJ: Pfeiffer, 2005.

6) **Create a Side Hustle—a small version of your business that you can do on the side, at the same time that you hold your current job.**
99 Side Hustle Business Ideas You Can Start Today: www.sidehustlenation.com/ideas/.

7) **Start your own business or nonprofit organization (note that there are hundreds of subcategories under this!).**
Guillebeau, Chris. *The $100 Start-Up: Reinvent the Way You Make a Living.* New York: Crown Business, 2012.

8) **Imagine your dream project (e.g., writing a book, collecting oral histories in your neighborhood, making a film, opening a show of your art at a local gallery). Then invite support from your friends or use an online crowdfunding platform like Indiegogo or Patreon to make it happen.**
Three of the most popular crowdfunding sites: indiegogo.com, patreon. com, kickstarter.com.

9) **Apply for a fellowship to be supported to do what you love. A few possibilities:**
Ashoka Fellowship program (social entrepreneurs): www.ashoka.org
Echoing Green Fellowship program (social entrepreneurs who are "innovators, instigators, pioneers, and rebels"): www.echoinggreen.org.
Hemera Foundation's Tending Space Fellowships for artists: hemera.org/for-artists.
Hemera Foundation's Contemplative Fellowships for health care professionals: hemera.org/cfhp.

10) **If you're an artist, begin selling your work on a site like Etsy. More possibilities:**

Set up your own online store through Shopify and keep more of the profits: www.shopify.com.

If you want to get started more quickly and you're okay with less profit for now, try one of these marketplace sites that take care of most of the details from printing to shipping:

Redbubble www.redbubble.com.

Society 6 www.help.society6.com.

Zazzle www.zazzle.com.

11) If you're a writer, self-publish your own book and sell it.

Friedman, Jane. "Start Here: How to Self-Publish Your Book." February 16, 2015: www.janefriedman.com/self-publish-your-book. An excellent overview of the process.

12) If you're a photographer, sell your photos to a site like Fotolia (www.us.fotolia.com). Other resources:

www.500px.com A photo community for discovering, sharing, buying and selling inspiring photography.

www.everythingmicrostock.com Helps photographers and artists start earning passive income. Use it to sell your photos, videos, animations, illustrations, music, sound effects, or other digital media online.

13) If you're a musician, head to your local town center and become a street performer.

Kettle, David. "Rules for Successful Buskers." *The Strad*, April 17, 2014. http://www.thestrad.com/rules-for-successful-buskers.

14) Join a time bank in your hometown, or organize one if it doesn't exist. Exchange your time and talents with others in your community, and help create a gift economy.

timebanks.org Learn the basics about how time banking works and find a time bank near you.

15) If you love to travel and have dreamed about living abroad: get trained to teach English to students in another country. And no, you don't necessarily need to know the language of the country to which you're moving.

William, Andrew. *TEFL: The Complete Guide to Teaching English Abroad.* CreateSpace Independent Publishing Platform, 2016.

16) If you love to travel and love being in nature: become a campground host for a season or longer. These are mostly volunteer jobs, but sometimes there is a stipend.

Camphost.org provides information about how to become a camp host and directory of open positions.

17) Become a house sitter as a way to travel the world for very little money, or simply live within your own community on a tight budget ... so you can free up more of your time to do what you love.

Nomador.com is a community-based platform that connects homeowners and house sitters.

APPENDIX A Loving Kindness Practice

Loving kindness, also called *metta*, is one of the oldest teachings and practices of Buddhism. This is the kind of love that is expansive and not based on any conditions or restrictions. We can freely offer it to friends, family, and all beings, including ourselves. While this may seem like a lofty ideal to realize, the Buddha taught that all of us have the potential to experience and offer this kind of love.

The Dhammapada, a collection of Buddhist teachings, includes this verse: "Hatred cannot coexist with loving kindness, and dissipates if supplanted with thoughts based on loving kindness." When you do this loving kindness practice on a regular basis, you begin to transform patterns of negativity and self-criticism into kindness and self-acceptance.

There are three steps in loving kindness practice. If you find it difficult to begin with the first step, it's okay to change the order and start with the second step (include the body scan described in step one). But do make sure to return to the first step at some point, as the capacity to direct loving kindness toward yourself is a prerequisite to being able to offer genuine kindness to others.

You can integrate loving kindness into your sitting meditation, but it can also be a stand-alone practice. Begin by sitting or lying down in a comfortable position.

Do a simple body scan, beginning with your toes and moving up through each part of your body. In a body scan, you pay attention to each part of your body, noticing any sensations that may be present, whether they are pleasant, unpleasant, or neutral. Just as you do with sitting meditation, try to bring a quality of nonjudgmental awareness to each section of your body. If, for example, you notice that your back is aching, you can say to yourself, "Back … Unpleasant," and breathe a bit more deeply into that part of your body. Then continue to move on.

As you arrive at your chest area, focus on your heart center. Breathe in and out from that area, as if you are breathing from your heart. Allow yourself to rest in this place for a few moments.

While you are breathing in and out from your heart center, notice any feeling of self-judgment or numbness that may arise, as well as any blockages, either physically or emotionally. If you identify such a feeling or blockage, again try to bring a quality of nonjudgmental awareness to that sensation. There is nothing "bad" about self-judgment or numbness, it is simply what is true for you in that moment.

As you continue breathing in and out from your heart, try to connect with a place within where you genuinely care for yourself, where you want to be safe and healthy. Know that this is the best kind of "selfish," the kind that enables you to offer your best work to the world.

Continuing to breathe in and out, say these phrases to yourself:

May I be free from harm.
May I be free from suffering and distress.
May I be safe.
May I be happy.
May I be able to live in this world with ease and joy.

Feel each phrase radiate through your whole body, mind, and heart.

In this second step, bring to mind a person for whom it is easy for you to feel unconditional love, someone who evokes the feeling of deep care and love, in an uncomplicated way. This may be a parent, grandparent, teacher, a dear friend, or it could even be a pet or animal friend.

As you hold this person or creature in your awareness, reconnect with your heart center. Repeat these phrases for this person or creature:

May they be free from harm.
May they be free from suffering and distress.
May they be safe.
May they be happy.
May they be able to live in this world with ease and joy.

Feel each phrase radiate through your whole body, mind, and heart.

Finally, in the third step you will practice sending this loving kindness to all beings, everywhere. Once again become aware of your heart center and come into contact with the kindness and warmth that you have been cultivating in the first two steps of the practice.

You are part of a vast network of life, one that includes humans, but also animals and plants, that is supported by the earth we all share, and by the elements of water, air, and fire. Allow yourself to feel this web of interconnectivity, and remember that all beings are your relatives.

Say each phrase silently to yourself:

May all beings be free from harm.
May all beings be free from suffering and distress.
May all beings be safe.
May all beings be happy.
May all beings be able to live in this world with ease and joy.

Feel each phrase radiate through your whole body, mind, and heart.

APPENDIX B Guide to Creating A Personal Retreat

A personal retreat is especially useful when you're in the midst of a big life transition, such as a career shift. During these times it can be easy to get thrown off track by others' expectations as well as by your own fears and hesitations. A personal retreat gives you a precious opportunity to reconnect with your wisdom and get more clarity on your next steps.

Several years ago, I gave myself the gift of a five-day personal retreat. While I have done many meditation retreats at Buddhist and other spiritual centers, that was the first time that I've taken myself through a solo process of my own design, and it was one of the most powerful experiences of my life. One benefit of doing your own retreat is that you can schedule it at a time that's most convenient for you (and it usually costs less money than going to a center).

If you're thinking of doing something similar, here are five ingredients that I found useful in putting together my retreat:

1. CHOOSE THE TIME AND SET YOUR INTENTION

The inspiration for my retreat came when I listened to a soft but insistent voice inside of me. That voice kept telling me that this was a critical time to create space in my life to pay attention to some recurring patterns and do some deep healing work around those patterns.

My gut feeling was that it would be great to take three months to do a retreat like this. That wasn't possible given the obligations of my life but when I thought about it, five days seemed like a stretch and yet realistic. I realized I could take that time right after Christmas and before New Year's Day. I didn't have to work then, and the quiet of winter was the perfect time to turn my attention inward.

So step number one was to commit that time to myself, to write it down in my calendar just like I would for an appointment with someone else, and then to protect those days and not schedule anything else during that time. That was a challenge! In fact, just being able to stick with that intention and promise to myself felt like one of the most powerful pieces of the process.

Your retreat doesn't need to be five days long. I was pretty lucky to be able to set that much time aside. Even dedicating one day for this purpose can be transformative—it's more about quality than quantity.

Your intentions will be unique to you but the important thing is to spend time to get clear on them before beginning your retreat. These intentions will inform the schedule and kinds of activities that you design for yourself.

One possibility for an intention is to focus on one or more of the chapters of this book and work through the exercises included in them. You may want to use your retreat time to create your Personal Mission Statement. Or, you might want to cast the net wider and give yourself space to explore other parts of your life beyond work (which will, of course, inform your work). Here are a few questions that may be helpful in uncovering your intentions for this retreat time:

- What is missing from my life that would truly nourish me?
- Where do I notice myself falling back into old, unhealthy patterns that I would like to transform, once and for all?
- What energy would I like to call into my life?

- What promises do I need to make to myself in order to live life to the fullest?

2. REMOVE DISTRACTIONS

One of the biggest reasons that retreats can have such a powerful impact is that we take ourselves out of the flow of our usual tasks and become responsible for just one thing: being present to ourselves.

To support this process, it's important to remove distracting elements during retreat time. This might mean letting people know that you won't be checking phone messages or emails (and giving them a way to reach you in case there is a bona fide emergency).

In my case, it also meant staying off of the computer and social media. While I did go online once during the first few days to check on an appointment I had made for later that week, I was pretty strict with myself about staying away from Facebook. By the end of the five days, I was amazed at the level of clarity that I experienced, and I'm certain that had to do with keeping myself in a distraction-free container. If you're able to refrain from time on the computer and other devices during your retreat, I highly recommend it.

3. CREATE A SACRED SPACE

When you establish a sacred space, you are creating a physical anchor that helps you return to your contemplative practice throughout your retreat. This space usually takes the form of an altar that you can set up somewhere in your home. If you do your retreat somewhere else besides home, bring altar supplies with you.

I created my altar on the first day and then continued to add to it as my retreat progressed. The altar was oriented to the four directions, each of which has an element associated with it: water for the South, earth for the West, air for the North, and fire for the East. I made sure that each direction on my altar had that element or at least a symbol of that element included in that quadrant: there was a candle in the east, a photo of a bird in the north, a cup of water in the south, and a stone in the west.

My altar was also populated with photos of special people in my life, feathers, tarot cards, and various other sacred objects. Ganesha, the Hindu elephant god, is a personal favorite of mine, so I had a couple of Ganesha statues protecting the whole altar.

Throughout each day of my retreat, I came back to this altar to sit in meditation, write in my journal, create collages, and simply dwell in the beauty of what I had created. It became my focal point and helped me to collect and express my energy throughout the five days.

As you go through your retreat time, you will most likely spend it in a variety of places but you can use this sacred space as your "returning home" location whenever you feel you need it.

4. DESIGN A STRUCTURE AND SCHEDULE

One thing I quickly discovered was that I needed to give myself a clear structure for each day and not be in a freefall about how to spend the time. While my schedule was more spacious and flexible than might have been the case if I had gone to a retreat center, it was still very important to have some kind of structure to follow.

Before the start of my retreat I drafted a schedule and taped it to the wall of my living room. Here's what it looked like:

6:30	Wake up
7:00	Zazen
7:30	Gentle stretching with music
8:00	Walk Lucy (my dog!)
8:45	Shower/body time
9:00	Breakfast
10:00	Session I
Noon	Lunch
2:00	Session II
3:30	Nap, reading, friend check-ins, bodywork
5:30	Dinner
7:00	Journaling
End of night Zazen	

This written schedule served as a visual reminder of what was going to happen next and helped to ground me when things felt a bit "out there." Before you begin your retreat, take time to come up with a schedule that feels doable for you. It's not set in stone and you can adjust it as the days go by, but it's very helpful to have it as a starting point.

What did I do in those morning and afternoon sessions? I integrated a variety of modalities that I had some experience with, including journaling, collage making, Authentic Movement, and shamanic journeying. In some sessions I chose a particular question to focus on and then explored it through movement. A couple of times I took a walk up to a hillside near my home and did a tarot card reading there to get more insight into my question. During one session, I wrote down the "false beliefs" that had begun to reveal themselves to me through my explorations, things like "I am not enough," and "I am a boring person, people don't want to be around me." I kept a pile of blank slips of paper and jotted these beliefs down as I noticed them. Near the end of the five days, after I had done a good deal of examining each of those beliefs to understand where they had come from and how they impacted my life, I had a ceremony of release and burned them in my fireplace. That felt great!

For your sessions, make use of whatever modalities speak to you: yoga, meditation, drawing, singing, movement, and journaling are just some of the possibilities. You may want to start by giving some sessions a specific theme based on the 6 Keys in this book, such as "What is my Core Intention?" or "How do I value my time and my gifts?" Some of the exercises included in this book can be included in your flow of activities, if that feels right to you. It can also be interesting to leave other sessions open and then see what your intuition tells you is important to focus on as you move through your retreat time.

5. SET UP A SUPPORT SYSTEM

Depending on your intentions, you may want to bring other people into the design of your retreat to support you.

In my case, I set up the first three days to have a lot of solo time, as that felt like an important way to uncover some old beliefs through dreamwork and shamanic journeying.

During the last two days of the retreat, I planned check-ins with a few trusted friends and healers, usually once a day. Sometimes I did these via Skype calls, one day my massage therapist came to give me some in-home energy work, and one day I went out for an appointment with my therapist.

You may choose to do your retreat entirely on your own, which is a wonderful thing. But if you have an intuition that it might help to invite the support of some dear friends, that is a great thing too. Again, take a look at your intentions and see what will best serve them in your retreat time.

Dear Brenda,

[Begin with a personal note to the recipient]

Over the past few months I have wrapped up a couple of client projects and have some room in my schedule as well as the need to generate some income. I'm reaching out to some folks who know me well and are familiar with my skills. I wonder if you are aware of individuals, groups, or organizations who may benefit from what I have to offer.

What I bring to the table...

- Community builder ... this is in my DNA! I love nurturing groups of people into a cohesive whole, drawing on our indi-

232

vidual gifts to create a collective something that is bigger than what any of us could do by ourselves. I do this through various mediums—in person, online, and combinations of both.

- Group facilitation
- Coaching, particularly for those who are going through a life/professional transition
- Marketing and fundraising know-how from more than two decades of work in the nonprofit sector
- Qualitative research—training and practice as an ethnographer and graduate degree in cultural anthropology gives me the tools to conduct insightful program evaluations as well as help teams to identify hidden assumptions that may be at play in their interactions. Bringing these assumptions to "light" can help to make for more effective teamwork.
- Strategic thinking from the heart
- Writing and editing

Beyond those skills, perhaps the most valuable thing I have to offer is that I believe in lifting other people up and creating the conditions so they can shine in their work. That gives me much more joy than taking the spotlight for myself. If I were in a band, I'd be your bass guitarist—laying down a strong foundational beat so that everyone can improvise beautifully and yet stay together.

If you know of any people or projects that might be a good fit for me, feel free to tell them about me, and please let me know! Ideally I am looking for contract or part-time work so I can continue to focus on writing my book.

I so much appreciate your support, and please let me know if there is any way I can support your good work.

Warmly,
Maia

ACKNOWLEDGMENTS

While writing is very much a solo endeavor, I've learned that it takes a village to create a book. Every book represents the coming together of resources of all kinds, including emotional, spiritual, and material. As I consider the many forms of support I've received in the process of writing this one, I realize it's impossible to name everyone who has played a part in its creation.

Recognizing that this list will be incomplete, I want to offer particular gratitude to everyone who has participated in the Fall in Love with Your Work online course since its inception in 2011. It's been a joy to witness you go through the transformative journey of discovering how to create livelihood that feeds both heart and soul. This book wouldn't have come into existence without your experiences and your willingness to share them so openly. I am especially grateful to those participants whose stories are shared at length in this book: Lauren Ayer, Katya Lesher, Lyndon Marcotte, and Leslie Rinchen-Wongmo. And to Jami Sieber and Yael Raff Peskin—while you weren't enrolled in Fall in Love with Your Work, your inner and outer journeys to create work that matters beautifully exemplifies the spirit of this process. Thank you all for your generosity in sharing your stories.

A deep bow to Dharma teachers and friends who have supported me to ground my life in the teachings of the Buddha and to understand what it means to practice right livelihood, especially Shosan Victoria Austin and Roshi Joan Halifax. To Sharon Salzberg and Mirabai Bush, thank you for your kind encouragement early on in this book-writing process, as well as your own skillful efforts to bring mindfulness into the workplace.

My "Wisdom Circle" (a far better name than "Mastermind"!), comprised of Ursula Jorch, Leslie Rinchen-Wongmo, and Lisa Wilson—our bimonthly conversations over the past years and your consistent encouragement have been essential ingredients to help bring this book into the world.

Pam Slim, thank you for being a fabulous mentor in how to run a business with integrity and joy, and for your generosity in contributing the foreword to this book.

Gratitude to Hisae Matsuda, my gifted editor at Parallax Press, who gently encouraged me to include more of my story in the manuscript, and to Ruby Privateer, for her skillful suggestions and copyedits. I am thankful to Rachel Neumann, publisher at Parallax, whose confidence in the idea for this book strengthened my confidence in writing it.

Arnie Kotler and Susan Moon, two mentors who taught me a great deal about the art of writing and editing—I feel so blessed to have met both of you early on in my own livelihood journey! Thanks as well to Kristin Barendsen, a dear friend and talented writer who provided invaluable editorial feedback on the first version of my book proposal.

To each person who became a patron through my crowdfunding campaign—your financial support made it possible for me to take the time necessary to nurture this book from an idea to a full-fledged manuscript.

Nannette and Chuck Overley, you provided an inspiring space in northern New Mexico where I could dive deep into a writing retreat. A good deal of these pages took shape during that time in your beautiful home—thank you.

Finally, one of my greatest treasures is my circle of friends scattered around the world. Three in particular have played an essential role in this process.

Gina Horrocks, thank you for being my heart's best friend, and for supporting and encouraging me through many "Big Leaps." I am forever grateful.

Katya Lesher, thank you for being my beloved cocreator in designing spaces for people to renew themselves, and for your editorial input throughout this book (especially for help in thinking through the "dance steps" that appear in chapter 11). We have much great work to do together!

Kristi Markey, thank you for our long friendship, and for your emotional and material support throughout this process. It means the world to me.

May the merit of this book benefit all beings!

ABOUT THE AUTHOR

Maia Duerr is a writer, organizational consultant, and coach for people going through life and career transitions. She draws on her years of Zen meditation practice and training in anthropology to create powerful tools for integrating mindfulness into the workplace and in clients' everyday lives. Through her workshops, retreats, online programs, and individual coaching, Maia has supported hundreds of people around the world to start or deepen a contemplative practice, and to create work that matters.

"How can I create work that I love?" has been her life's guiding question. After a ten-year career as a mental health professional, Maia received a MA in social and cultural anthropology from the California Institute of Integral Studies. As former Executive Director of the Buddhist Peace Fellowship, Research Director of the Center for Contemplative Mind in Society, and Director of Upaya Zen Center's Buddhist Chaplaincy Training Program, she has worked at the intersection of meditation, social justice, and cultural transformation for decades.

Maia lives in Santa Fe, New Mexico, where she enjoys long walks through juniper- and piñon-covered hills with her magical dog Lucy, and connecting with the land and culture of this place she calls home.

 **PARALLAX PRESS**

Parallax Press is a nonprofit publisher, founded and inspired by Zen Master Thich Nhat Hanh. We publish books on mindfulness in daily life and are committed to making these teachings accessible to everyone and preserving them for future generations. We do this work to alleviate suffering and contribute to a more just and joyful world. For a copy of the catalog, please contact:

Parallax Press
P.O. Box 7355
Berkeley, CA 94707
parallax.org